INTRODUCING
ISSUES WITH
OPPOSING
VIEWPOINTS®

# The Surveillance State

Lisa Idzikowski, Book Editor

GREENHAVEN
PUBLISHING

Published in 2022 by Greenhaven Publishing, LLC
353 3rd Avenue, Suite 255, New York, NY 10010

**Library of Congress Cataloging-in-Publication Data**

Names: Idzikowski, Lisa, editor.
Title: The surveillance state / Lisa Idzikowski, book editor.
Description: New York : Greenhaven Publishing, 2022. | Series: Introducing
  issues with opposing viewpoints | Includes bibliographical references
  and index. | Contents: The surveillance state | Audience: Ages 12–15 |
  Audience: Grades 7–9 | Summary: "Anthology of diverse viewpoints that address the
  questions of whether the US is operating under a surveillance
  state; can we have safety without surveillance; and whether it is too
  late to turn back from our present situation"– Provided by publisher.
Identifiers: LCCN 2020050946 | ISBN 9781534508033 (library binding) | ISBN
  9781534508026 (paperback)
Subjects: LCSH: Privacy, Right of–United States–Juvenile literature. |
  Domestic intelligence–United States–Juvenile literature. | Electronic
  surveillance–United States–Juvenile literature.
Classification: LCC JC596.2.U5 S835 2022 | DDC 323.44/820973–dc23
LC record available at https://lccn.loc.gov/2020050946

*Manufactured in the United States of America*

Website: http://greenhavenpublishing.com

# Contents

Foreword                                                              5

Introduction                                                         7

## Chapter 1: Is the US Operating Under a Surveillance State?

1.  America Is Becoming a Surveillance State                         11
    *C. Mitchell Shaw*
2.  Video Surveillance Has Evolved Over the Years                    17
    *Bob Mesnik*
3.  Bulk Surveillance Violates the Rights of Ordinary Citizens       23
    *Amnesty International*
4.  Thinking About Privacy Is Part of Modern Life                    28
    *Lee Rainie and Maeve Duggan*
5.  The Global Surveillance Industry Operates Without
    Accountability                                                   35
    *Privacy International*
6.  Crime Cameras May Not Be Worth the Investment                    40
    *David Lepeska*

## Chapter 2: Can There Be Safety Without Surveillance?

1.  Americans Are Concerned About Privacy and Security               47
    *Shiva Maniam*
2.  Surveillance Cameras Should Complement, Not Substitute
    for, Police                                                      52
    *Future Learn*
3.  If Done Correctly, Surveillance Systems Reduce Crime             57
    *Kevin McCaney*
4.  Privacy Is Not the Same As Having Nothing to Hide               61
    *Vrinda Bhandari and Renuka Sane*
5.  Surveillance Cameras Are a Governmental Intrusion into Our
    Private Lives                                                    66
    *Bill Newman*
6.  Integrity Could Improve the Surveillance Society                 72
    *Steve Mann and Joshua Gans*

## Chapter 3: Does High-Level Surveillance Threaten Americans' Liberty?

1. Surveillance Helps the NSA Spy on Americans                          79
   *Electronic Frontier Foundation*
2. American Attitudes About Privacy Are Conflicted
   and Divided                                                          84
   *Pew Research Center*
3. Privacy Claims Often Clash with the First Amendment                  91
   *Judith Haydel*
4. The Public Deserves Surveillance Transparency                        97
   *Dave Maass*
5. Facial Recognition Technology Can Be Used for
   Good Reason                                                          101
   *Marcia Wendorf*
6. Americans Are Fighting Their Governments Over Facial
   Recognition Surveillance                                            105
   *Nathan Sheard*


Facts About the Surveillance State                                      110
Organizations to Contact                                                112
For Further Reading                                                     114
Index                                                                   117
Picture Credits                                                         120

# Foreword

Indulging in a wide spectrum of ideas, beliefs, and perspectives is a critical cornerstone of democracy. After all, it is often debates over differences of opinion, such as whether to legalize abortion, how to treat prisoners, or when to enact the death penalty, that shape our society and drive it forward. Such diversity of thought is frequently regarded as the hallmark of a healthy and civilized culture. As the Reverend Clifford Schutjer of the First Congregational Church in Mansfield, Ohio, declared in a 2001 sermon, "Surrounding oneself with only like-minded people, restricting what we listen to or read only to what we find agreeable is irresponsible. Refusing to entertain doubts once we make up our minds is a subtle but deadly form of arrogance." With this advice in mind, Introducing Issues with Opposing Viewpoints books aim to open readers' minds to the critically divergent views that comprise our world's most important debates.

Introducing Issues with Opposing Viewpoints simplifies for students the enormous and often overwhelming mass of material now available via print and electronic media. Collected in every volume is an array of opinions that captures the essence of a particular controversy or topic. Introducing Issues with Opposing Viewpoints books embody the spirit of nineteenth-century journalist Charles A. Dana's axiom: "Fight for your opinions, but do not believe that they contain the whole truth, or the only truth." Absorbing such contrasting opinions teaches students to analyze the strength of an argument and compare it to its opposition. From this process readers can inform and strengthen their own opinions, or be exposed to new information that will change their minds. Introducing Issues with Opposing Viewpoints is a mosaic of different voices. The authors are statesmen, pundits, academics, journalists, corporations, and ordinary people who have felt compelled to share their experiences and ideas in a public forum. Their words have been collected from newspapers, journals, books, speeches, interviews, and the internet, the fastest growing body of opinionated material in the world.

Introducing Issues with Opposing Viewpoints shares many of the well-known features of its critically acclaimed parent series, Opposing

Viewpoints. The articles allow readers to absorb and compare divergent perspectives. Active reading questions preface each viewpoint, requiring the student to approach the material thoughtfully and carefully. Photographs, charts, and graphs supplement each article. A thorough introduction provides readers with crucial background on an issue. An annotated bibliography points the reader toward articles, books, and websites that contain additional information on the topic. An appendix of organizations to contact contains a wide variety of charities, nonprofit organizations, political groups, and private enterprises that each hold a position on the issue at hand. Finally, a comprehensive index allows readers to locate content quickly and efficiently.

Introducing Issues with Opposing Viewpoints is also significantly different from Opposing Viewpoints. As the series title implies, its presentation will help introduce students to the concept of opposing viewpoints and learn to use this material to aid in critical writing and debate. The series' four-color, accessible format makes the books attractive and inviting to readers of all levels. In addition, each viewpoint has been carefully edited to maximize a reader's understanding of the content. Short but thorough viewpoints capture the essence of an argument. A substantial, thought-provoking essay question placed at the end of each viewpoint asks the student to further investigate the issues raised in the viewpoint, compare and contrast two authors' arguments, or consider how one might go about forming an opinion on the topic at hand. Each viewpoint contains sidebars that include at-a-glance information and handy statistics. A Facts About section located in the back of the book further supplies students with relevant facts and figures.

Following in the tradition of the Opposing Viewpoints series, Greenhaven Publishing continues to provide readers with invaluable exposure to the controversial issues that shape our world. As John Stuart Mill once wrote: "The only way in which a human being can make some approach to knowing the whole of a subject is by hearing what can be said about it by persons of every variety of opinion and studying all modes in which it can be looked at by every character of mind. No wise man ever acquired his wisdom in any mode but this." It is to this principle that Introducing Issues with Opposing Viewpoints books are dedicated.

# Introduction

*"The fact is, conduct most of us think of as private and anonymous is increasingly taking place under the electronic gaze of video surveillance cameras."*

*—A Special Report by the New York
Civil Liberties Union, Fall 2006*

A sick child receiving treatment in the hospital. Excited travelers checking in to board their plane or to their hotel. Hungry teens grabbing a bite at their favorite fast food place. A young woman trying on makeup virtually. A law enforcement officer working to solve a missing persons case. These are all examples of times when different types of surveillance technologies are already in use. Companies are producing and refining these technologies. At the same time, organizations devoted to civil liberties are fighting the expansion of this technology, while some US states and cities are drafting legislation to prohibit its use.

Merriam-Webster defines "surveillance" as "the act of carefully watching someone or something especially in order to prevent or detect a crime," or "close and continuous observation or testing." In the examples given above, the use of surveillance technology could be arguably seen as positive or providing some benefit to an individual or group. But many individuals and organizations argue that common uses of surveillance have stepped beyond appropriate bounds.

Surveillance is a complicated issue. Americans express mixed views about the subject. According to a Pew Research survey, 14 years after the September 11 terrorist attacks, 54% of Americans said they disapproved of the government collecting their telephone and internet data (a type of surveillance) in the name of protection from terrorists. In the same study, almost three of every four people surveyed said they did not want to give up freedom or privacy for the sake of safety. Not surprisingly, about eight in ten adults said it was perfectly right to monitor communications of suspected terrorists.

Individuals are not the only ones weighing in. The American Civil Liberties Union (ACLU) is an organization actively watching surveillance trends. This group rigorously defends the rights that are given to people through the US Constitution, and it argues that surveillance takes away constitutionally guaranteed rights. The ACLU points to 2002, just after the September 11 attacks, when President George W. Bush signed an order giving the National Security Agency the power to spy on US citizens and other legal residents through recorded phone calls and intercepted emails. The ACLU argued that this act violated the Fourth Amendment to the Constitution, which states that Americans' privacy cannot be invaded without a warrant based on probable cause. Supporting this was a 1967 US Supreme Court decision that ruled Fourth Amendment protections include that from government eavesdropping.

So, where does this leave things? The government isn't the only entity collecting massive amounts of data from US residents. Think about all the businesses that function with the help of data. Telecommunications, retail and wholesale sales, and health care depend on the collection of personal data. A majority of Americans want to be in control over their own data, but few believe that they really are. Who hasn't experienced the uncomfortable feeling of seeing an ad on social media and realizing that they had been using an internet search about that very same product or topic a short time ago? In 2019, about 64% of all adults said they had seen ads or solicitations pop up based on their personal data. It certainly feels like someone is watching.

Businesses would argue that they need to use a variety of surveillance techniques to offer better service to their customers. They also might argue that it helps to prevent theft or shoplifting in brick and mortar stores. But is that stepping over the line of privacy? Not long ago, disguised employees would wander around the store keeping an eye out for shoplifters. Now, surveillance cameras scan every inch of stores in the hope of discouraging unwanted actions by customers.

A big question is whether all this surveillance is effective. Are terrorist activities really being prevented? Are crimes being prevented? Do mistakes occur when law enforcement agencies use surveillance? The short answer is yes … and no. In China, facial recognition surveillance is successfully being used to find children who have been abducted or trafficked. Imagine the relief when a parent is reunited with a long-lost child.

Surveillance cameras are being installed all over cities large and small. Studies done in big cities like Chicago, Illinois, and Washington, D.C., show that surveillance cameras in some areas do lessen the amount of crime. But this does not happen across the board in all locations. It seems to depend how the surveillance is used by police and how quickly law enforcement responds. And what about terrorists or those committing mass shootings? Experts contend that giving camera time to these individuals may not deter their activities but may in fact encourage it. And another unfortunate situation occurs when mistakes are made with these technologies. Facial recognition has helped find missing persons and those who commit crimes. But it has also caused people to be mistakenly identified, charged, and prosecuted for crimes they did not commit.

So, should surveillance be used? Should the technology be allowed to permeate society? Are people too worried about surveillance? Is the United States becoming a surveillance state? Are there positive aspects to the expanding world of surveillance? The current debate surrounding this topic is worthwhile and complex. *Introducing Issues with Opposing Viewpoints: The Surveillance State* offers a variety of diverse viewpoints written by experts in the field, shedding light on this interesting and ongoing contemporary issue.

# Chapter 1

# Is the US Operating Under a Surveillance State?

*Advances in technology have allowed for greater surveillance capabilities.*

# America Is Becoming a Surveillance State

*"Mass surveillance is the best tool against terrorism, and unless you have something to hide...it shouldn't bother you."*

### C. Mitchell Shaw

In the following viewpoint, C. Mitchell Shaw argues that the high degree of surveillance that has occurred since 9/11 is not necessary and is in fact harmful. The author contends that surveillance is eroding freedoms in American life and will potentially get worse. Shaw maintains that Americans have been conditioned to accept a loss of freedom and liberty and should resist these encroachments. C. Mitchell Shaw is a freelance writer who specializes in issues dealing with privacy, liberty, and the US Constitution.

**AS YOU READ, CONSIDER THE FOLLOWING QUESTIONS:**
1. What was one immediate result after 9/11, according to the viewpoint?
2. According to the author, has surveillance stopped terrorism?
3. Identify a type of surveillance as stated in the viewpoint.

"9/11: The Rise of the Surveillance State," by C. Mitchell Shaw, *The New American*, September 11, 2016. Reprinted by permission TheNewAmerican.com.

On September 11, 2001, nineteen al-Qaeda terrorists hijacked four airliners and flew three of them into the Pentagon and the Twin Towers of the World Trade Center. The fourth plane, which was reportedly headed to the White House, crashed in a field in Pennsylvania. By days end, almost 3,000 souls had perished and another 6,000 people were injured. The New York city skyline and the American political landscape were both changed. Fifteen years later, it appears that another casualty of that day was privacy. The Twin Towers came down and the surveillance state rose.

Almost immediately after 9/11, a series of events demonstrated that the power-brokers and insiders in Washington never let a tragedy go to waste. The USA Patriot Act was signed into law on October 26, 2001—just six weeks after the attacks and while Americans were still reeling from the shock. The Department of Homeland Security (DHS) began as the Office of Homeland Security two weeks before the Patriot Act was signed and was made official on November 25, 2002. In the meantime, more and more surveillance cameras began appearing on street corners and government buildings. Under the newly enacted Patriot Act, warrantless wiretapping and surveillance of everything from phone calls to texts to e-mails to Internet browsing histories to which books were checked out from the library became the standard tools of government in the "war on terror." Anyone who spoke out against the rising surveillance state was quickly accused of not understanding the danger of terrorism or—worse—siding with the terrorists.

In the 15 years since that dreadful day, the surveillance state has risen to a level unimagined by most at the time. Just a brief look at the last two years is enough to cause any concerned patriot to be worried about where the surveillance hawks are taking America. In December of 2014, Judge Richard Posner—a Reagan appointee to the Seventh Circuit Court of Appeals who has been called the most cited legal scholar of the 20th century by *The Journal of Legal Studies*—said the NSA should have free range to "vacuum all the trillions of bits of information that are crawling through the electronic worldwide networks," adding that the only reason anyone would have for objecting is that they are "just trying to conceal the disreputable parts of [their] conduct."

*Almost immediately after the devastating 9/11 terrorist attacks, the US government ramped up surveillance efforts.*

In his comments—which were made, ironically, during a panel discussion on "The Future of the Fourth Amendment" at the Georgetown University Law Center's conference, *Cybercrime 2020: The Future of Online Crime and Investigations*—Judge Posner went on to say, "Privacy interests should really have very little weight when you're talking about national security," because "the world is in an extremely turbulent state—very dangerous."

What is unfortunately conspicuous about Posner's comments is that they are not conspicuous at all. Instead, they fit right in with the steady diet of surveillance propaganda being fed to the American mind by politicians, bureaucrats, and the media. That message is two-fold: mass surveillance is the best tool against terrorism, and unless you have something to hide (in other words, unless you are a terrorist) it shouldn't bother you. Of course both of those points are demonstrably false.

First, mass surveillance is a lousy tool for fighting terrorism for several reasons. For one, terrorists use their own "home-grown" encryption tools for circumventing surveillance. For another thing, if the NSA, FBI, CIA, and other three-letter-agencies are looking for needles in haystacks, adding more hay is not a solution. By focusing their surveillance on any and all, the surveillance hawks limit their chances of actually fighting terrorism to something like lottery odds.

Second, plenty of ordinary non-terrorists have "something to hide." In fact, everyone does. It's why we have curtains and blinds over our windows. It's why we use envelopes for our letters. We know, deep down, that our private lives should stay private. What happens when you need to do an Internet search for an embarrassing medical question? What about a private, intimate text to your spouse? What about that phone call where you argue with your spouse? We do these things in private because they are private. And they ought to stay that way.

And, just to put in the for-what-it's-worth column, mass surveillance has not stopped major terror attacks in even recent years with the surveillance state operating overtime. In fact, think of the attacks right here in America in the past few years: the 2013 Boston Marathon bombing, the 2014 Garland, Texas shooting at the "Draw Muhammad" cartoon exhibit, the 2015 Chattanooga shootings at military recruiting stations, the 2015 San Bernardino shootings, the 2016 shootings at an Orlando, Florida nightclub, the ambush style murders of police officers across the country including those in

Dallas, Texas and Baton Rouge, Louisiana. Not to mention the hundreds of terrorist attacks in other parts of the world including France, Germany, the Philippines, the United Kingdom, and almost everywhere in the Middle East. If mass surveillance is the answer, why has it failed to uncover and prevent these attacks? Even with what almost everyone now knows about the state of the surveillance state in the wake of both the revelations made by Ed Snowden three years ago and the subsequent leaks and reports since then, CIA Director John Brennan said the attacks on Paris last year were the result of *too little surveillance*. Too much, it appears, is never enough for the surveillance hawks. Even when it doesn't work, they can't admit the simple fact that it can't work, they simply say more is needed.

What mass surveillance has managed to accomplish—at least in large part—is the erosion of the idea of privacy and liberty. Many Americans have come to accept the practices of being stripped (whether literally or digitally) or groped before being allowed to board a plane. Many have come to expect that their every web search, e-mail, phone call, text, and other communications will be logged and monitored. In fact, a report released last year by the Pew Research group revealed that fifty-five percent of the experts surveyed by the report do not believe that there will be an infrastructure of privacy rights within the next decade. Only 45 percent believe things will get better.

So, while terrorism—and the war on terrorism—continues, surveillance is becoming the norm. Police departments all over the nation are using cell-site simulators to vacuum up all mobile phone traffic within range, in violation of the Fourth Amendment. The NSA and other agencies routinely capture all communications and web traffic. The federal government has ended the cease-fire in the Crypto-Wars and is seeking to circumvent or outright ban the technology which allows private communications.

The mantra in the months following 9/11 was "If we (fill in the blank), the terrorists have won!" This was used to try to convince Americans to buy new cars, build houses, take vacations, and accept the surveillance that was increasing (but was not fully understood until Snowden). The truth though, is that if we accept the surveillance state, the terrorists have won. Consider the chilling words of terrorist leader Osama bin Laden who, in an interview with Al-Jazeera in the weeks after 9/11, gloated, "I tell you, freedom and human rights in America are doomed." He added, "The US government will lead the American people in—and the West in general—into an unbearable hell and a choking life."

On the 15th anniversary of the day America changed, Americans who still care about liberty and privacy must redouble their efforts to maintain and restore those God-given rights. Because the alternative is that the legacy of 9/11 will be bin Laden's "unbearable hell" and "choking life" under constant surveillance.

## EVALUATING THE AUTHOR'S ARGUMENTS:

Viewpoint author C. Mitchell Shaw presents an argument against an increase in surveillance. Do you agree with Shaw's argument, or do you think that surveillance does prevent terrorism? What points does the author make that helped you reach your conclusion?

Viewpoint

2

# Video Surveillance Has Evolved Over the Years

**Bob Mesnik**

In the following viewpoint, Bob Mesnik gives readers an overview of surveillance systems from its early start. The author provides an overview of how surveillance technology has changed and the groups of individuals using surveillance technology. Bob Mesnik is the president and owner of Kintronics, a company that provides surveillance and security systems.

*"In the US, commercial surveillance applications began around 1947."*

**AS YOU READ, CONSIDER THE FOLLOWING QUESTIONS:**
1. What is an early type of surveillance equipment mentioned in the viewpoint?
2. Was black and white or color better for surveillance, according to the author?
3. What are the two general types of surveillance equipment, as mentioned in the viewpoint?

"The History of Video Surveillance," by Bob Mesnik, Kintronics, July 20, 2016. Reprinted by permission.

F rom the early beginnings of closed circuit television (CCTV), it was somewhat controversial. It was designed to increase our security and safety, but does it threaten our privacy? How has video surveillance changed over the years? This article reviews the history of surveillance and how it has evolved into a technology that has become part of our lives.

## History

Video surveillance is not new; it has been around for quite a while. One of the first recorded applications for closed circuit television system (CCTV) was back in 1942. It was used to view the launch of V2 rockets in Germany. In the US, commercial surveillance applications began around 1947. In 1957 a number of companies such as General Precision Labs (GPL division), provided CCTV camera systems for education, medical and industrial applications.

Early CCTV equipment and TV broadcast equipment shared technology. Both camera systems supported grey-scale video (not color) and measured and defined performance using NTSC standards. Note the USA used NTSC (525 lines at 60 fps) while Europe used PAL (625 lines at 50 fps). A camera with 525 vertical scan lines actually had only 480 visible lines.

There is a difference between scan lines and lines of resolution. The TV line of resolution is defined as one black and one white line, so the actual resolution was less than 240 TV lines of resolution.

To measure resolution, the camera was pointed at the EIA-1956 resolution chart which was viewed on a monitor (with hopefully better resolution than the camera). It primarily measured the horizontal resolution because the vertical resolution was restricted by the fixed number of vertical lines (525 in NTSC). This was a very subjective measurement, because TV engineers determined the maximum resolution as the point where they could not discern converging lines.

Color cameras became available in the 1950s, and there was a debate on whether or not color was better for surveillance. Black-white (or grey-scale) cameras provided better resolution and low light sensitivity, while color made it easier to identify someone by the clothes they were wearing.

*CCTV security cameras are installed in some school classrooms, ostensibly for protection.*

The early camera systems were primarily used for real time viewing, because of the lack of reliable video recording systems. There was some reel to reel tape solutions available from Sony and Ampex, but they were not easy to use. The introduction of videocassette recorders (VCR) in 1970 led to the increased popularity of video surveillance.

## Evolution of Technology
The introduction of network attached IP cameras was a significant technology change for the CCTV industry. Axis introduced the first IP cameras in 1996. These new cameras used the Ethernet network for communication rather than coax cable. Video signals were now sent as digital encoded signals instead of analog signals.

The new communication method proved to be a difficult concept for the older analog security dealers to handle. It took a while for the new technology to become popular. It was only after computer dealers (who understood computers and networks) started selling IP camera systems that the market began to grow.

The first IP cameras provided 4CIF (704 x 480 pixels) or VGA (640 x 480 pixel) resolution. This was similar video resolution to the older analog cameras. One of the first megapixel IP cameras was introduced in 2002 by IQinvision. This 1.3 megapixel (1280 x 1024 pixels) cameras provided over four times the resolution of the older VGA cameras. Other companies, such as Arecont Vision, introduced 2-megapixel cameras in 2004. The high resolution of the IP camera provided a dramatic improvement over the older analog camera technology.

It took some time for the traditional CCTV camera manufacturers to get on board with the new IP technology. By 2003, major surveillance camera companies such as Samsung, Sony, and Panasonic started to embrace the new technology. By 2007 they developed high performance, megapixel IP cameras. Even though Axis dominated the market because of their early entry, the new megapixel IP cameras from the CCTV companies quickly outperformed the Axis cameras. For example, Samsung (Hanwha Techwin) and Sony developed IP cameras with better performance that are priced more aggressively. Take a look at our camera review, which describes the results of our testing.

By 2014 there were more IP cameras sold than analog surveillance cameras. Today, it is estimated that over 30 million surveillance cameras are used in just the United States, with over 100 million cameras worldwide (analog and IP cameras). It's amazing how far we have come in the last 20 years.

## The Changing Market

Today there are a very wide range of IP cameras available. The market is now split between low-cost consumer grade cameras, and professional surveillance cameras.

## Consumer Cameras

In 2011, lower cost cameras were introduced by large Chinese camera companies such as Hikvision and Dahua. These lower performance IP cameras have led to a dramatic increase in home IP surveillance systems.

Lower cost IP camera systems and ease of installation have made it possible for large organizations to self-install instead of relying on CCTV installers. This has dramatically changed the market and increased the number of IP surveillance camera systems

## High Performance Professional Cameras

In the last couple of years high performance IP cameras were introduced for the professional security market. This included ultra-high resolution cameras, those with better low light and wide dynamic range, and those that included very long range lenses.

In 2015 very high resolution 4K cameras were introduced. Sony was one of the first to develop the sensor required for this new class of camera. 4K camera specifications are somewhat confused because the term was originally used for the display of video on TVs and monitors. IP cameras that provide at least 4,000 horizontal pixels are considered to be 4K, but there are actually a number of different 4K IP cameras available. For example, there is the 8-megapixel Axis 1428, the Samsung 12-megapixel SNB-9000 camera, and the 20-megapixel SNC-VM772R camera from Sony. All considered 4K cameras, but all with different capability.

It is important to note that these very high resolution cameras require much better lenses than are used in the lower resolution cameras. Be careful, when you see a relatively low priced 4K camera, you are probably not getting the best lens. The lenses for these cameras are a significant part of the overall cost of the camera and can cost well over $2,000. If you find an IP camera that costs under $1,000 it probably won't provide the resolution you expect.

High performance cameras also include very long range IP cameras that can view objects that are miles away in total darkness. Not only can IP cameras be used for typical surveillance applications, they can be placed on top of mountains to help detect forest fires, or placed underwater to view sea life.

## More Than Just Surveillance

Surveillance is everywhere, and it's growing in popularity. Now almost anyone can install IP camera systems. Camera systems watch our homes, schools, businesses and cities. They are being used by law enforcement agencies around the world. When we watch the news today, we are not surprised to see video from the latest robbery or terror attack. Surveillance has also become part of our mobile world. Anyone with a smart phone is now able to capture video.

Is this pervasive surveillance good or bad? The American Civil Liberties Union (ACLU) continues to be concerned about public privacy. In spite of these concerns, the general feeling is that surveillance is helping us become more safe and secure. Today CCTV is no longer "closed circuit" it is available to all of us, and it is improving our safety and security. Not only does it help law enforcement arrest villains, it also helps to make our lives safer.,

**EVALUATING THE AUTHOR'S ARGUMENTS:**

In this viewpoint, Bob Mesnik concludes that surveillance is available in many forms and is probably good for all of us. Do you agree with this? Why or why not?

# Bulk Surveillance Violates the Rights of Ordinary Citizens

*"The information collected and stored by the Government can reveal the most intimate aspects of a person's private life."*

**Amnesty International**

In the following viewpoint, Amnesty International argues a case against the use of surveillance in the United Kingdom. This case was brought on by whistleblower Edward Snowden's shocking revelations concerning global government surveillance programs. The viewpoint states that surveillance is wrong in a democratic society. Amnesty International is a globally based organization that campaigns for social justice and equal rights for all people.

"UK's Surveillance Powers to Be Considered by Europe's Highest Human Rights Court," Amnesty International, July 8, 2019. Reprinted by permission.

AS YOU READ, CONSIDER THE FOLLOWING QUESTIONS:
1. According to the viewpoint, which agency does the UK share its surveillance with?
2. Are surveillance practices legal as analyzed by the author?
3. What is the Investigatory Powers Tribunal as explained by the author?

The UK Government's bulk surveillance powers will be examined by the highest chamber of the European Court of Human Rights this week, the latest stage in a long-running legal battle over the UK's unlawful use of previously-secret surveillance powers and its sharing of massive amounts of private communications.

On Wednesday (10 July), the Grand Chamber of the European Court of Human Rights—the court's highest body—will hear arguments from Amnesty International, Liberty, Privacy International and other human rights organisations from four continents over the unlawfulness of the UK's bulk surveillance practices.

The case is the culmination of six years of revelations and legal challenges following Edward Snowden's disclosure in 2013 of how the UK's GCHQ intelligence agency was secretly intercepting and processing millions of private communications of ordinary people on a daily basis, and—without a clear legal foundation or proper safeguards—sharing data with the USA's National Security Agency, as well as other countries' intelligence agencies.

Last September, a lower chamber of the European Court of Human Rights ruled that UK laws enabling mass surveillance were unlawful, violating rights to privacy and freedom of expression. The court observed that the UK's regime for authorising bulk interception was incapable of keeping the "interference" to what is "necessary in a democratic society."

However, Amnesty and others then asked the court's Grand Chamber to go further by entirely rejecting the UK's overtly bulk surveillance regime.

Lucy Claridge, Amnesty International's Director of Strategic Litigation, said:

*Edward Snowden blew the whistle on the UK's far-reaching surveillance operations.*

"Exposed to the light of day, some of the UK's industrial-scale surveillance practices have already been found unlawful, but Europe's highest human rights court could now decide to entirely do away with dragnet surveillance and unfettered transnational sharing of millions of people's private data.

"We need to be protected from intrusive and over-powerful states that think nothing of secretly harvesting and sharing vast amounts of our private data and communications."

## UK Surveillance Case Before the Grand Chamber

The Grand Chamber has been asked to rule that the mass interception, processing and storage of private communications is not compatible with the rights to privacy and freedom of expression. Should it decide to endorse last year's ruling, the Grand Chamber has been asked to update "minimum safeguards" over government-led surveillance—given "the state's ability to extract, on an enormous scale, sensitive and personal information from intercepted material." The Grand Chamber has also been asked to rule that the UK's

intelligence-sharing arrangements with foreign intelligence agencies are inadequate and violate people's rights to privacy and freedom of expression.

## Parties in the Case

The case is the culmination of three original legal challenges from the following groups and individuals: the American Civil Liberties Union, Amnesty International, Bytes for All, the Canadian Civil Liberties Association, the Egyptian Initiative for Personal Rights, the Hungarian Civil Liberties Union, the Irish Council for Civil Liberties, the Legal Resources Centre, Liberty and Privacy International, Big Brother Watch, Open Rights Group, English Pen and Dr. Constanze Kurz, the Bureau of Investigative Journalism and Alice Ross.

Amnesty and nine other applicants are represented by Ben Jaffey QC and Gayatri Sarathy of Blackstone Chambers, and David Heaton of Brick Court Chambers.

## Snowden's Revelations

The present case began in 2013, following Edward Snowden's revelations that GCHQ was secretly intercepting, processing and storing data concerning millions of people's private communications, even when those people were clearly of no intelligence interest (the "Tempora" programme). Snowden also revealed that the Government was accessing communications and data collected by the USA's National Security Agency and other countries' intelligence agencies.

All of this was taking place without public consent or awareness, with no basis in law and with no proper safeguards. The information collected and stored by the Government can reveal the most intimate aspects of a person's private life—where they go, who they contact, which internet sites they visit and when.

In 2014, the Investigatory Powers Tribunal—the highly secretive UK court which hears claims against GCHQ, MI5 and MI6—ruled that these practices may in principle comply with the UK's human rights obligations. This was the finding subsequently challenged in the European Court of Human Rights, which partly ruled against the UK last year.

In the course of its proceedings, the Investigatory Powers Tribunal found that UK intelligence agencies had unlawfully spied on the communications of Amnesty and South Africa's Legal Resources Centre. It also found that UK intelligence sharing with the US, which had been governed under a secret legal framework, was unlawful until disclosed during the proceedings.

## EVALUATING THE AUTHOR'S ARGUMENTS:

In this viewpoint, Amnesty International presents a case against surveillance practices in the United Kingdom. Does the author agree with the author of the first viewpoint? Use specific examples from both viewpoint articles to back up your argument.

# Thinking About Privacy Is Part of Modern Life

*"Is it worth it to hand over my personal information in exchange for something else?"*

**Lee Rainie and Maeve Duggan**

In the following viewpoint, Lee Rainie and Maeve Duggan analyze the issue of surveillance and what Americans believe about this topic. The authors contend that Americans have varying thoughts about privacy and surveillance. The authors present evidence that shows that a basic level of distrust exists among the American public. They suggest that a generational difference may surround feelings about surveillance. Lee Rainie is the director of technology and internet research at the Pew Research Center, and Maeve Duggan is a former research associate at Pew.

**AS YOU READ, CONSIDER THE FOLLOWING QUESTIONS:**
1. According to the viewpoint, where do Americans feel they are being surveilled?
2. Are surveillance cameras acceptable as stated in this viewpoint?
3. Are people hopeful about privacy concerns, according to the authors?

"The State of Privacy," by Lee Rainie and Maeve Duggan, Pew Research Center, January 14, 2016.

Americans frequently face choices about whether or not to share information about themselves in return for getting something that is potentially valuable to them. From retail stores that track customers' shopping behavior in exchange for discounts to online applications that offer free services in exchange for serving personalized ads to users, Americans regularly face the choice: Is it worth it to hand over my personal information in exchange for something else?

Of course, in some cases, people have little control over whether personal information about them is collected. As one respondent in the survey summarized:

> *I share data every time I leave the house, whether I want to or not. Every time I use a credit card, every time I walk in 80% of the commercial establishments in the nation, every time I drive down streets in most any city or town in the nation, I'm being recorded in some fashion. The data is there, and it's being used, and there isn't a damn thing most of us can do about it, other than strongly resent it. The data isn't really the problem. It's who gets to see and use that data that creates problems. It's too late to put that genie back in the bottle.*

Another made the point that bargaining over personal information seems a perpetual part of modern life: *"I continually have to decide how much personal information to share in return for prizes/ money."* Another added: *"Every day, the chance that your data is shared increases. All data are ultimately digitized."*

For the past two years, Pew Research Center surveys have mapped this complicated landscape and Americans' nuanced feelings about privacy and surveillance.

The surveys have found that Americans conjure an array of ideas when they think about privacy. They feel privacy is important in their daily lives in a number of essential ways, starting with the idea of not being under surveillance all the time and the appeal of being able to share ideas and secrets with others in a way that is unobserved. Yet, they have a pervasive sense that they are under surveillance when in public. Very few feel they have a great deal of control over the data that is collected about them and how it is used.

Moreover, Americans have low levels of trust in the government and business sectors that they associate with data collection and monitoring. They are not sure their core communications channels are secure, and they have exceedingly low levels of confidence in the privacy and security of the records that are maintained by a variety of institutions in the digital age. Indeed, noteworthy numbers of them have suffered privacy breaches, especially younger adults.

While some Americans have taken modest steps to stem the tide of data collection, few have adopted advanced privacy-enhancing measures. They are divided about the value of government surveillance programs aimed at thwarting terrorists. And majorities expect that a wide range of organizations should have limits on the length of time that they can retain records of their activities and communications. Additionally, they say it is important to preserve the ability to be anonymous for certain online activities.

In the online focus groups for this study, the theme of contingency came up in responses to each scenario. Asked about the acceptability of surveillance cameras at a workplace where some thefts had occurred, one respondent said:

> *It depends if the cameras are in public areas (i.e. hallways, public gathering areas, lobbies, etc.) and in storage areas where supplies or personal belongings are kept (i.e. closets, locker rooms, supply rooms) this would seem to be sufficient. Cameras that monitor personal work spaces would be invasive even to the most diligent employee with absolutely nothing to hide except perhaps a sneeze, a scratch, a clothing adjustment or just bending over wrong in front of the camera.*

Another respondent, explaining his answer about his physician inviting him to use an online medical records system, wrote:

> *It depends if I think the site is secure enough to put my information on. If it was a weak site with low development I would not use it. If it was high security like a bank site I would use it.*

*When you make an online purchase, do you worry about data collection?*

And yet another respondent, asked whether she would allow a tracking device placed on her car to monitor her driving habits perhaps leading to lower insurance payments, explained how these factors would shape her judgment:

> *It depends on how much the discount would be and what their privacy policy would be. I would not agree to it if the data is shared with anyone at all, and I would want it to be stored only temporarily and securely.*

## What's the public's mood? People's level of anxiety and hopefulness are all over the place

In light of these current and future concerns, participants in the focus groups were asked how much dismay or even anger they felt at the current state of things, and they offered a range of answers trying to pinpoint their level of concern.

*"It's hopeless."*

*"No, they are as bad as we make it sound."*

*"I'm not hopeless, just resigned."*

*"Loss of privacy is inevitable. I've accepted that."*

*"Nothing is completely safe. That's just life in these times."*

*"[Loss of privacy] is a major annoyance."*

*"Not hopeless, necessarily—I think that the landscape has so fundamentally shifted that we have an entirely new paradigm to deal with."*

*"I think people are not happy with everyone in their business."*

*"It's bleak about privacy—the more controls the government enables the less privacy we have. We have lost a lot of privacy in the US since 9/11 and are losing more every day, and it appears no one cares. The less freedom we have the less privacy we should expect."*

Some focus group participants tried hard to wrestle with the complexities of the subject, moving it beyond a binary situation of privacy or no privacy and speaking instead about how they tried to live out their views about privacy. A woman in one of the groups said: "Monitoring in public places is completely different from being monitored in your own home, or in your bank accounts, and god knows what else. I went off Facebook for several years just because I assumed everything was being collected about me, and I wanted to avoid that. And, of course, there's also the matter of leaving a record behind of your political and other views that could be detrimental in certain cases. For instance, if you apply for a job, and the employer thinks your opinions are too liberal."

**FAST FACT**

In 2019, seven in ten Americans said the security of their data had decreased in the previous five years.

## Some are concerned about the future of privacy; some have hope for a technological fix

In online focus groups tied to the most recent Pew Research Center survey, people were often downcast about the future of privacy, as were many experts who participated in a wide and diverse canvassing by the Center last year about the long-term fate of privacy. A sampler of some of the participants' views from the most recent research:

*"Our life has become an open book. What are you gonna do?"*

*"Privacy as we knew it in the past is already gone. Privacy in the future will be very different. We will have very little about our daily lives kept private. Our important records such as banking and medical will become tighter, likely through biometric access, but I expect the hackers to keep up with even that technology to obtain what they want."*

*"I think that there will be less and less privacy."*

*"It's an annoyance that will mostly be fixed."*

*"I think that the concept of 'privacy' no longer exists. I think it is more about 'informed consent.'"*

*"I think law abiding citizens sit back way too much. There are a multitude of things we should be demanding legislation about as it is."*

*"The future generation will ABSOLUTELY see privacy different. Millennials put EVERY aspect of their life on social media and have no concern for their personal or financial safety. I feel that we are in a place where we can decide how to keep our information private, but the more and more companies require information from us for access to an app, our email accounts or even our bank accounts, it will be unavoidable to not release some of our information. It is nothing to be hopeless about, rather we need to continue to be vigilant with whom we share our information and for those we do share our information with, we need to ask questions and ensure our own safety first. People need to get on board that privacy of information is a thing of the past."*

*"The law is way behind technology. Privacy was written for a non-digital world. Don't expect any privacy in the future."*

*"I think a backlash is coming against too much intrusion. Privacy services will become popular."*

## EVALUATING THE AUTHORS' ARGUMENTS:

In this viewpoint, it is clear that authors Lee Rainie and Maeve Duggan have presented opinions of everyday people. Does the issue of surveillance appear to affect people of all ages? Use specific examples from the viewpoint to support your answer.

# The Global Surveillance Industry Operates Without Accountability

*"Surveillance technology consists of a wide range of constantly developing sophisticated systems the very existence of which is kept secret."*

**Privacy International**

In the following viewpoint, Privacy International presents a detailed picture of the surveillance industry. The author examines who is involved with this industry, the products sold, the customers purchasing the equipment, and why it is a problem. Privacy International is an organization with global reach that works to promote the basic human right of privacy.

**AS YOU READ, CONSIDER THE FOLLOWING QUESTIONS:**
1. Who or what makes up the global surveillance industry, according to the author?
2. How is surveillance technology used as outlined in this viewpoint?
3. Why is surveillance technology an issue?

"The Global Surveillance Industry," Privacy International. Reprinted by permission.

Today, a global industry consisting of hundreds of companies develops and sells surveillance technology to government agencies around the world. Together, these companies sell a wide range of systems used to identify, track, and monitor individuals and their communications for spying and policing purposes. The advanced powers available to the best equipped spy agencies in the world are being traded around the world. It is a lucrative business, but is so secretive and murky that no-one really knows its overall value.

In 1995, Privacy International published Big Brother Incorporated, the first ever study of the increasing role of the arms industry in the international trade in surveillance technology and their role in exporting sophisticated surveillance capabilities from developed countries to non-democratic regimes. Since then, we have continued to monitor the industry, and have compiled our data within the Surveillance Industry Index (SII), the world's largest publicly accessible database on the commercial surveillance sector, featuring as of May 2016 data on 528 companies. Our report, The Global Surveillance Industry, provides a comprehensive analysis of the industry, including its history, products, and customers.

## Who's Involved?

The modern electronic communications surveillance industry evolved from the commercialisation of the internet and digital telecommunications networks during the nineties, when governments began passing new laws demanding new electronic surveillance powers and technical protocols to guarantee government access to networks. In response, a global industry developed consisting of arms contractors, telecommunications companies, IT businesses, and specialised surveillance companies, overwhelmingly based in large arms-exporting countries with advanced economies.

A nationwide surveillance architecture is comprised of various types of companies. Internet Service Providers (ISPs) and telecommunications operators, which manage networks and charge subscribers for certain services, such as internet, mobile and fixed-line telephony services, may be required to ensure that their networks are accessible to government agencies. Telecommunications equipment vendors are

*Global surveillance is a murky industry with little oversight.*

companies which develop the necessary hardware, such as switches and routers, upon which networks run. Because they are developed with Lawful Interception capabilities, when they are exported some equipment by default actively carries out surveillance, or is designed in a way to be easily accessible for surveillance purposes. Some vendors specially develop and market equipment for surveillance purposes. Surveillance companies sell technologies for law enforcement and intelligence purposes. These can be systems which facilitate the Lawful Interception process, sold for example to operators for compliance purposes, or sold directly to government agencies providing more widescale, untargeted, and intrusive capabilities.

## What Do They Sell?

When it comes to surveillance technology, you might think of small GPS tracking devices, cameras, and hidden bugs—and you'd be right. But it also consists of a wide range of constantly developing sophisticated systems the very existence of which is kept secret. This includes equipment used to monitor internet communications on a mass nationwide scale, malware deployed through national internet providers which can turn on your computer or mobile's camera, and mobile phone monitoring technology which can trick hundreds of mobiles into connecting to it, used for example to identify everyone at a protest.

## Who Do They Sell It To?

The industry and its customers stubbornly refuse to disclose any details about sales. Information that we have only comes from investigative reporting by journalists and NGOs and some export data published by a handful of governments. From what we know, government agencies ranging from customs and tax enforcement to foreign intelligence are buying their surveillance equipment from the market, in countries with the most advanced agencies to some of the most authoritarian countries in the world.

## Why Is This an Issue?

The spread of the internet and new communications methods has increased the intrusiveness of surveillance as well as its power. It's now technically possible to monitor entire groups and nations on a mass scale, systematically and relatively cheaply. This poses a fundamental threat to individuals' security, civil society, human rights, as well as democracy itself.

Even in political systems with significant checks and balances, surveillance capabilities have regularly outstripped the ability of laws to effectively regulate them. In non-democratic and authoritarian countries, surveillance technology can be used for human rights abuses and undermine democratic development and privacy, a human right essential in allowing individuals control, dignity, and the realisation of other human rights such as freedom of expression. The global surveillance industry has sold such systems to some of the world's worst human rights abusers, where they have been targeted at human rights activists, journalists, opposition members, and the judiciary. Activists have had their communications read to them during torture.

## What Can Be Done?
The industry continues to operate without accountability because it refuses transparency. Surveillance companies market their products to government agencies behind closed doors at arms fairs closed to the public, and refuse to reveal any information about their customers.

Privacy International, together with journalists and researchers around the world, investigate and expose this secret world, providing information on which companies are involved, what they are selling, who they are selling them to, and how their technology is being used. We advocate for strong safeguards in international export control laws which can stop exports if there is a risk of human rights abuses and force governments to provide more transparency. We promote strong international and national laws to provide sufficient safeguards against abuses and that surveillance is only conducted in line with international human rights law and with strong oversight. But most importantly we work with an international network of experts and advocates to build a global movement capable of holding government surveillance powers and the industry which facilitates them to account.

**EVALUATING THE AUTHOR'S ARGUMENTS:**

Viewpoint author Privacy International presents a case of control over surveillance technology. Construct an argument either for or against the control of surveillance technology using specific details from the viewpoint.

**Viewpoint 6**

# Crime Cameras May Not Be Worth the Investment

*"The successful model for getting the alleged 'bad guy' is more Sam Spade than Jack Bauer."*

### David Lepeska

In the following viewpoint, David Lepeska argues that surveillance cameras don't always do their job. As such, they may not give communities a return on their investment. Surveillance cameras are expensive to purchase, install, and maintain. Although they can be effective in terms of helping law enforcement solve crimes, quite frequently it comes down to tried-and-true methods such as eyewitness accounts and community policing. David Lepeska is a freelance journalist who has contributed to the *New York Times*, the *Guardian*, and the *Atlantic*, among other news organizations.

**AS YOU READ, CONSIDER THE FOLLOWING QUESTIONS:**
1. What led to the capture of the would-be terrorist in Times Square?
2. How much has London's surveillance camera system cost to install and maintain, according to the viewpoint?
3. What is the monetary "cost" of murder?

"Are Crime Cameras Really Worth the Money?" by David Lepeska, Bloomberg, December 12, 2011. Reprinted by permission.

I n May 2010, a 30-year-old Pakistani-American drove his Nissan Pathfinder into one of the most scrutinized urban spaces on the planet and parked along the curb.

In the hours that followed, more than 80 city surveillance cameras—as well as dozens of private cameras, constant media feeds and amateur tourist videographers—failed to capture an image of Faisal Shahzad and his suspicious, fertilizer-packed SUV in Times Square. All those electronic eyes couldn't even provide police investigators an image of the suspect (the balding middle-aged man standing near the vehicle in popular security footage had nothing to do with the case).

Instead, a street vendor pointed out the smoking Pathfinder to mounted police officers, leading to Shahzad's capture more than 50 hours later. In the end it wasn't high-tech 21st century surveillance that caught the crook, but good old-fashioned community vigilance. "The successful model for getting the alleged 'bad guy,'" wrote the *Boston Globe*, "is more Sam Spade than Jack Bauer."

For years, video surveillance has been seen as a potent weapon in the fight against urban crime. The Department of Homeland Security lays out millions of dollars to throw a surveillance net on our cities. Last year, it spent more than $830 million in 64 metropolitan areas as part of its Urban Area Security Initiative—up from $15 million and seven cities for the same program in 2009. This year the total is $662 million across 31 cities.

Their best advice is to manage expectations about the impact of crime camera systems: "Footage quality may be adversely impacted by darkness, inclement weather, equipment damage or dirt"; "Images can be grainy, cloudy, or otherwise unclear"; and "cameras may be diverted to another viewable area when an incident occurs and catch little or nothing of the incident itself."

Yet the question of effectiveness has haunted governments, police officials and academic researchers for decades. It should also haunt taxpayers, because camera surveillance doesn't come cheap. London's 10,000 camera system, for example, has cost more than $320 million to set up and maintain.

The answer, thus far, has been decidedly mixed. Studies in San Francisco and London—two cities on opposite sides of the camera-density spectrum—found little to cheer. San Francisco's

*Do expensive surveillance cameras reduce crime more effectively than tried-and-true methods used for decades?*

68 cameras placed in high-crime areas failed to reduce assaults, sex offenses and robbery, and merely moved murder down the block, according to a UC-Berkeley report.

London city data revealed that police were no more likely to catch the perpetrators of crimes committed in camera-dense areas than in other boroughs, suggesting no link between more cameras and better crime solving.

A 2009 meta-analysis by researchers from Northeastern University and the University of Cambridge examined 44 previous studies and turned up some positive results. They found surveillance systems to be most effective in parking lots, cutting crime by 51 percent. Cameras in public transport areas—at subway stations, on trains and at bus stops—generally reduced crime by almost one quarter. And camera systems in public settings cut crime by about seven percent.

Britain—with as many as 4 million cameras across the country—accounted for the majority of these reductions.

Now comes a rigorous new study from the Urban Institute, analyzing surveillance systems in Chicago, Baltimore and Washington, D.C. The Department of Justice's Office of Community Oriented Policing Services (COPS), which has invested more than $16 billion to advance community policing at the state and local levels since 1994, sponsored the study, released in September.

The researchers focused on select high crime areas where cameras had recently been installed and studied crime statistics going as far back as 2001 to include before and after data. In Baltimore, crime fell by 25 percent in one area, 10 percent in another and yet stayed the same in a third. In Washington, cameras appeared to have no effect on criminal activity.

In Chicago, the country's most extensive, integrated network, cameras in Humboldt Park correlated to a 12 percent decline in overall crime, including a 33 percent reduction in drug offenses and robberies and a 20 percent drop in violent crime. Meanwhile, a second Chicago area of study, West Garfield Park, saw no crime drop.

The Urban Institute researchers made two important advances over previous studies. First, they reviewed each city's decision-making process, the set-up of the surveillance system and finally usage. They found that active monitoring by trained personnel had a greater impact than cameras merely left to record video for later use, in the event of a crime in that area. They also found that costs, if not monitored, can spiral out of control.

Second, the researchers devised a system for calculating the social and governmental costs of various crimes, including expenses related to arrest, pre-sentencing, incarceration and cost to victim. "No prior research has sought to explore the degree to which camera use is cost-beneficial—a critical inquiry in light of the economic challenges currently being experienced by jurisdictions across the country," they wrote in the executive summary.

Under their system, murder costs $1.4 million, aggravated assault $89,000, robbery $120,000 and rape just $62,000. Baltimore saved $1.50 for every dollar spent on crime cameras, according to the report. The crimes prevented in Humboldt Park saved Chicago a whopping $4.30 for every dollar spent on both the Humboldt and West Garfield systems.

In the end, the Urban Institute researchers offer a handy guide for city officials and law enforcement agencies, with tips from the reasonable ("assess your needs and budget before investing,") to the mundane ("weigh the costs and benefits of using active monitoring").

Aaron Doyle, a criminologist at Carleton University who is part of the Surveillance Studies Centre at Queen's University and co-editor of a book out next month called *Eyes Everywhere: The Global Growth of Camera Surveillance*, sees this study as consistent with previous work.

"The worst-case scenario is that these positive results in two of the three cities will be over-hyped and lead to the kind of mega-expensive runaway train that CCTV has been in Britain," says Doyle. "It is possible that a modest well-planned network could be part of a range of measures that would help in some limited contexts, but I think crime is better dealt with in ways that build and involve community."

**EVALUATING THE AUTHOR'S ARGUMENTS:**

Viewpoint author David Lepeska cites opinions of experts that the success of surveillance cameras might be overstated. Can you see where such surveillance might not be a one-size-fits-all solution? Where could surveillance cameras work and where might they fail?

# Chapter 2

# Can There Be Safety Without Surveillance?

11:23:30

*Would you trade personal privacy for security if it made the streets safer?*

Viewpoint

1

# Americans Are Concerned About Privacy and Security

*"People are more aware that greater and greater volumes of data are being collected about them."*

**Shiva Maniam**

In the following viewpoint, Shiva Maniam maintains that the American public is concerned about their right to privacy and security of personal data. The author notes that this concern might depend on what is happening at the time in the outside world. People's views of news reports of terrorism appear to have an impact on the responses of surveyed Americans. Maniam presents a balanced argument showing the feelings of Americans in respect to a complicated issue often affected by world events. Shiva Maniam is a former research assistant at the Pew Research Center.

**AS YOU READ, CONSIDER THE FOLLOWING QUESTIONS:**
1. What connection do terror attacks have with privacy?
2. How did Edward Snowden's revelations immediately impact Americans' views on privacy and data collection?
3. What may happen over time to people's attitudes, according to the viewpoint?

"Americans Feel the Tensions Between Privacy and Security Concerns," by Shiva Maniam, Pew Research Center, February 19, 2016.

Americans have long been divided in their views about the trade-off between security needs and personal privacy. Much of the focus has been on government surveillance, though there are also significant concerns about how businesses use data. The issue flared again this week when a federal court ordered Apple to help the FBI unlock an iPhone used by one of the suspects in the terrorist attack in San Bernardino, California, in December. Apple challenged the order to try to ensure that security of other iPhones remained protected, and also to provoke a wider national conversation about how far people would like technology firms to go in protecting their privacy or cooperating with law enforcement.

Events have had a major impact on public attitudes on this issue. Terrorist attacks generate increased anxieties. For instance, the San Bernardino and Paris shootings in late 2015 had a striking impact. A Pew Research Center survey in December found that 56% of Americans were more concerned that the government's anti-terror policies have not gone far enough to protect the country, compared with 28% who expressed concern that the policies have gone too far in restricting the average person's civil liberties. Just two years earlier, amid the furor over Edward Snowden's revelations about National Security Agency surveillance programs, more said their bigger concern was that anti-terror programs had gone too far in restricting civil liberties (47%) rather than not far enough in protecting the country (35%).

At the same time, there are other findings suggesting that Americans are becoming more anxious about their privacy, especially in the context of digital technologies that capture a wide array of data about them. Here is an overview of the state of play as the iPhone case moves further into legal proceedings.

## How People Have Felt About Government Anti-Terror Policies

Pew Research Center surveys since the 9/11 terrorist attacks have generally shown that in the periods when high-profile cases related to privacy vs. security first arise, majorities of adults favor a "security first" approach to these issues, while at the same time urging

*Data breaches at Target and other big box stores have eroded consumer confidence.*

that dramatic sacrifices on civil liberties be avoided. New incidents often result in Americans backing at least some extra steps by the law enforcement and intelligence communities to investigate terrorist suspects, even if that might infringe on the privacy of citizens. But many draw the line at deep interventions into their personal lives.

For instance, our survey shortly after the 9/11 attacks found that 70% of adults favored requiring citizens to carry national ID cards. At the same time, a majority balked at government monitoring of their own emails and personal phone calls or their credit card purchases.

It should be noted that surveys have also found that people's immediate concerns about security can subside over time. In a poll conducted in 2011, shortly before the 10th anniversary of 9/11, 40% said that "in order to curb terrorism in this country it will be necessary for the average person to give up some civil liberties," while 54% said it would not. A decade earlier, in the aftermath of 9/11 and before the passage of the Patriot Act, opinion was nearly the reverse (55% necessary, 35% not necessary).

When the *New York Times* reported in late 2005 that President George W. Bush authorized the NSA to eavesdrop on Americans, subsequent Pew Research Center surveys found that 50% of

Americans were concerned that the government hadn't yet gone far enough in protecting the country against terrorism, and 54% said it was generally right for the government to monitor the telephone and email communications of Americans suspected of having ties with terrorists without first obtaining court permission. Some 43% said such surveillance was generally wrong. Quite similar numbers were found in a survey when President Barack Obama took office in 2009.

Right after the Snowden revelations in June 2013, a Pew Research Center poll found that 48% of Americans approved of the government's collection of telephone and internet data as part of anti-terrorism efforts. But by January 2014, approval had declined to 40%.

And many Americans continue to express concern about the government's surveillance program. In an early 2015 online survey, 52% of Americans described themselves as "very concerned" or "somewhat concerned" about government surveillance of Americans' data and electronic communications, compared with 46% who described themselves as "not very concerned" or "not at all concerned" about the surveillance.

## How People Feel About Corporate Practices

As businesses increasingly mine data about consumers, Americans are concerned about preserving their privacy when it comes to their personal information and behaviors. Those views have intensified in recent years, especially after big data breaches at companies such as Target, eBay and Anthem as well as of federal employee personnel files. Our surveys show that people now are more anxious about the security of their personal data and are more aware that greater and greater volumes of data are being collected about them. The vast majority feel they have lost control of their personal data, and this has spawned considerable anxiety. They are not very confident that companies collecting their information will keep it secure.

**FAST FACT**

In 2016, the NSA collected over 151 million phone call records from Americans.

## In Assessing Public Attitudes, Context Matters—and So Does How the Question Is Framed

One consistent finding over the years about public attitudes related to privacy and societal security is that people's answers often depend on the context. The language of the questions we ask sometimes affects the way people respond.

A recent Pew Research Center study showed that, in commercial situations, people's views on the trade-off between offering information about themselves in exchange for something of value are shaped by both the conditions of the deal and the circumstances of their lives. People indicated that their interest and overall comfort level in sharing personal information depends on the company or organization with which they are bargaining and how trustworthy or safe they perceive the firm to be. It also depends on what happens to their data after they are collected, especially if the data are made available to third parties, and on how long the data are retained.

A study in the wake of the Snowden revelations showed that there was notable change in public attitudes about NSA surveillance programs when questions were modified. For instance, only 25% favored NSA surveillance when there was no mention of court approval of the program. But 37% favored it when the program was described as being approved by courts. Similarly, characterizing the government's data collection "as part of anti-terrorism efforts" garnered more support than not mentioning this (35% favored vs. 26% favored).

> **EVALUATING THE AUTHOR'S ARGUMENTS:**
>
> Viewpoint author Shiva Maniam explains how Americans feel about data collected by communication systems. From what you've read so far, do you think that these feelings differ according to what kind of surveillance is being done (camera vs. phone data)? Why or why not?

# Surveillance Cameras Should Complement, Not Substitute for, Police

*"It may be that the number of surveillance cameras must be sufficiently high in order to achieve their full crime-reducing potential."*

**Future Learn**

In the following viewpoint, Future Learn presents information and analysis on the question of whether surveillance cameras really are the best way to reduce crime. The analysis also asks if surveillance alone reduces crime, or if the crime reduction—when it happens—is due to a combined effort between the actions of surveillance and an increased police presence. According to the author, statistical analysis is not clear-cut. Future Learn is an online educational platform.

**AS YOU READ, CONSIDER THE FOLLOWING QUESTIONS:**
1. In the studies used by the viewpoint, does surveillance alone always reduce crime?
2. Where did new surveillance equipment reduce crime, according to the author?
3. What is the best scenario for crime reduction as concluded by the viewpoint?

Under the rational choice model of crime, police reduces crime by increasing the expected probabilities of arrest and punishment.

But having a larger police force is not the only way to achieve this. Surveillance technology, such as street surveillance cameras (CCTVs) and dashboard cameras, can also deter crime by increasing the probabilities of arrest and punishment, at a fraction of costs of hiring more officers. Can cameras be a more cost-effective alternative in reducing crime?

In light of a rapid growth in surveillance cameras in recent years, many researchers investigated whether the use of surveillance cameras reduces crime. However, there is no clear consensus yet. Criminologists Brandon Welsh and David Farrington reviewed 44 existing studies on the effect of surveillance cameras on crime and found that the evidence is mixed: 15 found that cameras significantly reduce crime, 3 found that cameras significantly increase crime, and 23 found no significant effect of cameras on crime.

However, they note a few interesting patterns from existing findings.

First, most studies that find that surveillance cameras reduce crime (14 out of 15) are based on the U.K. data. Incidentally, the U.K. is one of the heaviest users of the surveillance cameras in the world (with an estimated number of cameras between 4 million and 6 million), and it may be that the number of surveillance cameras must be sufficiently high in order to achieve their full crime-reducing potential.

Secondly, existing studies show that the effect of surveillance cameras widely varies across different empirical settings. Specifically, research consistently shows that introducing surveillance cameras

*Along with surveillance cameras, the use of dashboard cams and bodycams by police officers is intended to reduce and deescalate crime.*

in (previously unattended) car parks leads to a large and significant crime reduction, while its effect on city and town centers, public transport, and public housing is more muted.

## Limitations

While these studies are certainly informative, there are several conceptual problems that limit our understanding of the causal effect of surveillance cameras on crime. One problem is that most policy interventions that bring new surveillance cameras to car parks, city centers, and public housing also bring other changes. For example, when a city government sets up new surveillance cameras in a large car park, this change is often accompanied by fencing, additional security staff, and improved street lighting. As a result, it becomes difficult to separate the effect of surveillance cameras from the effects of these other crime-prevention measures.

Perhaps a more fundamental challenge is that there are just so many different ways to set up and use security cameras. For example, suppose a researcher runs a regression analysis on how the number of surveillance cameras is related with crime rates, and concludes that increasing the number of cameras by 20 percent leads to a 5 percent reduction in crime. But how should these additional cameras be set up? Should they be close to each other so that the camera coverage would be complete, or should they be set up more sparsely to cover a larger area? Should they be set in places with high crimes or high traffic? A simple regression result cannot answer such questions.

One possible remedy to this problem is to use alternative measures of surveillance camera presence (other than the mere number of cameras) in regression analyses. For example, several studies use the coverage rate of the surveillance cameras (that is, how much of the target area is covered by surveillance cameras) in their empirical analyses. This is probably a better measure to assess the relationship between surveillance cameras and crime, but computing the rate of surveillance camera coverage is a lot more difficult than counting the number of cameras. (To compute the coverage rate, one would have to know exact views of each surveillance camera.)

Furthermore, many modern surveillance camera systems are equipped with advanced features, such as turning automatically toward the sound of gunshots and the ability to recognize people's faces and other objects, and the effect of these newer surveillance cameras are likely to be very different from the effect of older analog cameras. How can a simple regression analysis pick up this difference?

## Can Surveillance Cameras Be a More Cost-Effective Alternative to Hiring More Police?

Theoretically, the presence of more surveillance cameras on the streets should increase the probabilities of detection and arrest, and deter some potential criminals from offending. However, the effectiveness of surveillance cameras will be greatly compromised if there is no matching increase in the number of police officers and security managers who analyze the images and actually go out and catch criminals.

Thus, it is probably more appropriate to view surveillance cameras and police as complements instead of substitutes, and look for an optimal combination of cameras and officers which achieves the maximum crime-reduction given the available budget. Investments on other areas of crime prevention are also likely to be relevant. How effective would a surveillance camera be at night without proper lighting?

## EVALUATING THE AUTHOR'S ARGUMENTS:

In this viewpoint, author Future Learn presents a balanced opinion about the use of surveillance cameras and the reduction of crime. Have you been aware of surveillance cameras in a public space? If so, where, and did it make you feel safer? Why or why not?

# If Done Correctly, Surveillance Systems Reduce Crime

*"The presence of cameras was effective in reducing crime for some, though not all, areas."*

### Kevin McCaney

In the following viewpoint, Kevin McCaney argues whether surveillance cameras can reduce or prevent crime. McCaney provides evidence obtained from testing surveillance systems in three large metropolitan US cities. He continues his analysis by offering possible solutions to increase the effectiveness of surveillance systems aimed at preventing crime. Kevin McCaney is a former editor for GCN, an organization that provides information and analysis of IT systems to the governmental and educational sectors.

**AS YOU READ, CONSIDER THE FOLLOWING QUESTIONS:**
1. Which US cities are cited as testing sites in the viewpoint?
2. How has the surveillance technology been positive in the targeted areas, according to the author?
3. What aspect does the cost of this technology play in cities, as reported in the viewpoint?

Do surveillance cameras prevent crime?

Cities around the country have been installing camera systems in recent years, often funded by federal Homeland Security grants, and many have reported good results, but independent research on their effectiveness has been scarce, according to the Urban Institute.

So the institute, which does economic and social policy research, studied the surveillance systems in three cities—Baltimore, Chicago and Washington, D.C.—and recently issued a report on how they affected crime rates.

The verdict: The presence of cameras was effective in reducing crime for some, though not all, areas. The key isn't in just having cameras, the report states, but in how they're used— how many cameras are employed and where they're set up, how well they're monitored, and how well officials balance privacy concerns with utility.

In Baltimore, officials installed 500 cameras mostly in a 50-block downtown area, monitored by retired police officers in a control room, and saw crime rates drop steadily. In other neighborhoods, though, the results were mixed, the report states, dropping in some areas but not in others.

Chicago flooded its downtown with 6,000 cameras, paid for by a combination of federal, state and city funds. The institute's study focused on two neighborhoods, Humboldt Park and West Garfield Park, that had a combined 2,000 cameras. It found that crime rates dropped in one area but not the other. The report attributes the discrepancy to the fact that Humboldt Park, where crime decreased, had a higher concentration of cameras, and that West Garfield Park residents thought police weren't consistently monitoring the cameras.

Monitoring may have come into play in Washington, where cameras didn't have an impact on crime rates, the report states. After the District installed cameras in high-crime areas, residents raised privacy concerns, leading officials to restrict monitoring. The cameras can be monitored only from a control room where a police official with the rank of lieutenant or higher is present, an officer typically is watching feeds from four or five cameras at a time, and police are prohibited from monitoring people based on race, gender, sexual orientation and other factors.

*When deployed correctly, surveillance cameras seem to be effective in the reduction of crime in urban areas.*

Mixed results notwithstanding, the report concludes that the cameras are an effective tool in reducing crime if deployed the right way, and they can be worth the sometimes substantial investment in setting up the systems.

In Chicago, for instance, where crime dropped in one area but not in another, the institute's report determined that the city still saved $815,000 a month on "criminal justice costs and victims' financial and emotional costs," and that, "the crimes prevented in Humboldt Park saved the city $4.30 for every dollar spent on the surveillance system."

The report offers recommendations for helping to improve the chances of success with surveillance systems, including:

Balance utility with privacy. Residents must be protected from invasions of privacy, but rules that are too strict can limit the systems' effectiveness. In the areas in the study where crime rates didn't drop, police might not had had enough cameras and might not have been actively monitoring them.

Involve the community. Explaining the reasons for a surveillance system and getting community input from the start can help gain acceptance.

Don't underestimate costs. In all three cities, the costs of installing, maintaining and monitoring the systems was higher than officials originally thought.

Start small, and place cameras carefully. Beginning with a couple cameras lets police figure out how to best use them, before expanding the program.

Invest in active monitoring. Although 24-hour, active monitoring raises privacy concerns, Baltimore police said it gave them the best results, sometimes allowing officers to get to a crime in progress.

Train detectives and prosecutors. Video evidence not only helps police investigate crimes, it can be used as evidence in court. But it has its limits, particularly if a crime was recorded in bad weather or at night, or if the camera did not catch all of a crime because it was not being monitored. When monitoring, police can direct the camera, otherwise, it pans across an area. Baltimore prosecutors reported running into the "CSI effect," in which juries expect high-quality forensics and technical evidence, and might be influenced if video evidence shows only part of a crime because the camera panned away. The report recommends prosecutors be trained in the best ways to present surveillance footage as evidence.

## EVALUATING THE AUTHOR'S ARGUMENTS:

Viewpoint author Kevin McCaney suggests that training of police officers in the use of surveillance should help with effectiveness of this technology. In your opinion, would the author of the previous viewpoint agree with McCaney? Use specific details from each viewpoint to support your answer.

# Privacy Is Not the Same As Having Nothing to Hide

**Vrinda Bhandari and Renuka Sane**

*"As far back as 1890, privacy was understood as the 'right to be let alone,' a fact missed by the 'nothing to hide' paradigm."*

In the following viewpoint, Vrinda Bhandari and Renuka Sane contend that "having nothing to hide" is not a valid reason to invade privacy through surveillance. The authors maintain that everyone needs privacy to function as a healthy person. They argue that privacy and secrecy are different issues and should not be confused. Finally, the authors maintain that not having individual privacy should be cause for fear. Vrinda Bhandari is a lawyer. Renuka Sane is an economist. Both are writers for Live Mint.

**AS YOU READ, CONSIDER THE FOLLOWING QUESTIONS:**
1. What does the "nothing to hide" argument assume, as stated by the viewpoint?
2. How do privacy and secrecy differ, according to the authors?
3. What is the link between data collection and privacy, according to Bhandari and Sane?

"Privacy and the 'Nothing to Hide' Argument," by Vrinda Bhandari and Renuka Sane, Live Mint, August 9, 2017. Reprinted by permission.

The right to privacy hearings before the nine-judge bench of [India's] Supreme Court ended recently. During the conclusion, it was argued on behalf of the state of Gujarat that privacy claims are only made by those who have done something wrong.

Unfortunately, arguments such as these, namely the "I have got nothing to hide" argument, represent a common misconception of the meaning and value of the right to privacy. Under this view, only people with something to hide, or those who have done something wrong, are concerned about the loss of privacy. If you have nothing to hide, then information about you cannot really be used against you. Thus, the argument proceeds, no harm should be caused to you by the breach of your privacy.

But some harm is caused to us when our privacy is breached. It is why we draw curtains at our homes or keep private diaries. The right to one's privacy, family, home or correspondence, has long been recognized internationally. We do not want our neighbours, or the state, to know what happens inside our homes or inside our heads unless we choose to share that information with them. We cherish private spaces to do and be as we like, free from the gaze of others, and not because something immoral or illegal is transpiring inside our homes. The "nothing to hide" argument makes an incorrect moral judgement about the kinds of information people want to hide.

It also wrongfully equates privacy with secrecy, even though they are distinct concepts. Privacy is about exercising the choice to withhold information, which others have no need to know. Secrecy, on the other hand, is about withholding information that people may have a right to know.

As historian Jill Lepore explains, "Secrecy is what is known, but not to everyone. Privacy is what allows us to keep what we know to ourselves." The "nothing-to-hide" paradigm evaluates any breach of privacy only from the perspective of disclosure of unwanted information. Nevertheless, privacy is a much richer concept than secrecy. The right to privacy includes a bundle of rights such as the privacy of beliefs, thoughts, personal information, home, and property. In fact, as far back as 1890, privacy was understood as the "right to be let alone," a fact missed by the "nothing to hide" paradigm.

*Even if we have nothing to hide, the fundamental right to privacy is important to preserve.*

Today, privacy is regarded as central to our identity, dignity, ability to have intimacy, and meaningful inter-personal relations. It determines our interaction with our peers, society, and the state.

Privacy should thus be viewed as an integral part of self-development, a shorthand for "breathing space," since individual autonomy is all about the ability to control and share information selectively. For instance, we do not always want all of our friends to know everything about us.

But surely, you may ask, the government has a right to monitor its citizens' actions? After all, if you have "nothing to hide," then you should not worry about government surveillance. First, such an argument justifying mass surveillance upends the long-standing principle of presumption of innocence.

Second, it fundamentally misunderstands the consequences of the perceived loss of privacy and ensuing chilling effects on speech and behaviour. The fear that who we meet, what we say, and which websites we visit could be subject to scrutiny, may result in an unconscious change in (even lawful) behaviour. When we believe we are being observed, we are more likely to behave according to socially accepted norms. The change in behaviour, thus, has less to do with the content of our actions, but more to do with the knowledge of being watched.

Such a modification of behaviour is also evident in the arena of free speech and expression. A person critical of the ruling government may be more likely to self-censor her views if she believes her communications are being monitored. The reduction in diversity of views only undermines the democratic process.

Third, surveillance programmes are problematic even when there is no "undesirable" information that people want to keep hidden. Law professor Daniel Solove explains this beautifully by using the example of Kafka's *The Trial*, where the problem is not prohibited behaviour. Rather, it is the protagonist's exclusion from the judicial process, both in terms of knowledge or participation, and the attendant suffocating powerlessness and vulnerability created by the system's use of his personal data.

Finally, justifying the invasion of privacy because "I have nothing to hide" takes a short-term view of privacy and data collection. Data once collected can be used, misused, shared, and stored in perpetuity. Worse, it can be combined with other individually inconsequential data points to reveal extremely significant information about an individual. For example, mere knowledge that an unmarried woman went to a gynaecologist does not tell us much. But if we combine this information with a visit to an abortion clinic later, we suddenly know much more about her, and more than she may want to reveal publicly.

It is true that both the private sector and the state can know this information. But in the hands of the state, which has the monopoly on coercion and violence, it is far more potent.

# Fast Fact

According to Pew Research, 64% of Americans are concerned with the data collection activities of the US government.

The multiple dimensions of privacy seem to have been lost in the arguments put forward by the state opposing the recognition of the fundamental right to privacy. We may have nothing to hide, but if the arguments of the state are accepted, we will certainly have something to fear.

**EVALUATING THE AUTHORS' ARGUMENTS:**

In this viewpoint, Vrinda Bhandari and Renuka Sane make a compelling argument against the invasion of privacy. Do you agree or disagree? Use details from the viewpoint to support your view.

# Surveillance Cameras Are a Governmental Intrusion into Our Private Lives

**Bill Newman**

*"A lawbreaker who doesn't want his image captured simply will avoid the intersections with the cameras."*

In the following viewpoint, Bill Newman makes an argument against setting up surveillance cameras in the small northeastern city of Northampton, Massachusetts. The author notes that the measure will be ineffective in preventing serious crime. Perhaps more troubling, the surveillance footage could be used against ordinary citizens by various government agencies. Also, the addition of these "safety cameras" could have negative effects unique to small cities. Bill Newman is a lawyer with the ACLU of Massachusetts and writes for the *Daily Hampshire Gazette*.

"Columnist Bill Newman: The Case Against Surveillance Cameras," by Bill Newman, *Daily Hampshire Gazette*, March 11, 2017. Reprinted by permission.

Not in my town and not in my name.

That's my response to the surveillance cameras that the police have proposed to install permanently at the downtown intersections in Northampton. Here's why:

The cameras will not stop or prevent any crime as Police Chief Jody Kasper has made clear. As a law enforcement mechanism, they have extremely limited, if any, utility. A lawbreaker who doesn't want his image captured simply will avoid the intersections with the cameras.

On the other hand, the surveillance cameras would capture the image of every person in the major crosswalks of Northampton every minute of every day, which would then be stored for at least three weeks, and would be readily available to federal law enforcement upon request. ICE, the FBI, and Department of Homeland Security will all be able to apply their face recognition, biometric and lip reading technologies to those images. (So could the Northampton Police although the chief says they won't).

Fortunately, there is a surveillance limitation ordinance now pending before the City Council. That proposal would not ban all police use of cameras. Quite to the contrary, cameras would continue to be used in the parking garage and outside the police station, as well as in police vehicles and for large temporary events.

If enacted, the ordinance could be amended by the council at any time to respond to local needs. Even now as the proposal proceeds through the council's legislative process, its sponsors plan to amend it to specifically permit cameras for criminal investigations.

But the proposal would have one extremely important effect. It would stop the proliferation of this wholesale governmental intrusion

*The effectiveness of surveillance cameras installed in small towns is under debate. Many citizens believe it's not worth the threat to their privacy.*

into our private lives. While the City Council recently adopted a resolution against further deployment of downtown police cameras, a resolution, by definition, is nonbinding and aspirational only and has no legal teeth. In contrast, an ordinance has the force of law.

Proponents of this surveillance technology proclaim that there is no constitutional right to privacy in a public place. And there's some truth to that assertion—in the sense that when you're out in public, you can't claim to live in Harry Potter-land, wrapped in an invisibility cloak. But in the context of this proposal, the mantra of no privacy in a public space misses the point entirely.

Surveillance cameras would implement an enormous, constant and perpetual invasion of our privacy. Crossing the street in Northampton does not constitute our consent to the government creating and maintaining images and files of us and our friends and associates that can be shared with and retained by all law enforcement, local and federal, across America, forever.

Two related points: First, the ubiquity of private cameras does not mitigate or excuse the threat to civil liberties caused by such governmental surveillance. Second, such a profoundly deleterious change in the relationship between the residents of Northampton and the city police would have to be caused by some dramatic and compelling reasons. None have been offered.

I don't think it is too much to ask that Northampton not become the unabashed local leader in surveilling its citizens. As reported by the *Gazette*, the Easthampton and South Hadley police departments do not use surveillance cameras. In Belchertown, as in Northampton already, cameras are used in and around the police station. Belchertown has one additional camera on the town common.

In Amherst, there is one surveillance camera, other than those in the parking garage and the Senior Center, apparently trained on the location where drunk students do stupid drunk-student things.

Let's talk costs.

First, surveillance costs money, a lot of money. The price tag for the first year is $83,000. Costs would increase over time. So what are we talking about over the next decade: $1 million, $2 million?

Of course, after making the down payment for infrastructure in the first year, inertia and precedent would create enormous financial and practical pressure to maintain the system.

My suggestion for next year's $83,000 and the subsequent $1 million: If you want to promote community policing, make the city safer, and make people feel more secure downtown, why don't you use that money to put another patrol officer on the sidewalk or on a bike?

But the waste of taxpayers' dollars is only one of the costs. The surveillance technology would also hurt local businesses. Many visitors and residents alike will follow the maps that undoubtedly will be ubiquitously distributed, showing how to navigate downtown Northampton without being surveilled by law enforcement. Some businesses will be difficult to access, and they will lose customers.

And just imagine what our city will feel like with notices on each corner of the city's main intersection of Main, King and Pleasant streets: "Welcome to Northampton. You are being surveilled by law enforcement. All images available to the FBI, DHS, and ICE for at least three weeks. Enjoy your day." Some potential visitors will decline to visit or won't visit as often or stay as long. The same is true for residents.

But the biggest cost of this proposal would not be financial. The biggest cost would be the loss to our civic life caused by the shredding of our social fabric and the norms of Northampton.

"Paradise City!" I love our aspirational moniker. But a paradise city does not condone public officials sounding like George Orwell—as a few have recently—when they euphemistically describe the downtown surveillance cameras as "safety cameras."

For the past two months, public hearings, City Council debates and intense discussion in the local media have focused on this issue. Residents, elected officials, and public employees have spent hundreds, actually probably thousands, of hours in considering the City Council proposal.

Dismissing such civic engagement, some public officials now are claiming that notwithstanding all this time, effort, energy, focus and debate, the Northampton City Council should not even address the issue, but rather should kick the can down the legislative road for six months. They dismiss the importance of this community involvement and want the matter considered only as one aspect of the capital improvement part of the Police Department appropriation in the budget next spring. Seriously?

This position not only does a grave injustice to all who have devoted so much time and energy to figure out Northampton's public policy. It is, at its core, a terrible idea. Surveilling your citizens is not simply a budget item. It's a matter of policy and morality. The time to pass the surveillance nonproliferation ordinance is now. If and when the time should come for a different policy, the City Council can pass one.

A final note. Some people think they should not oppose the surveillance cameras because Jody Kasper floated this proposal, and they like Kasper and want to support her. But this reasoning is sophistry, and it's wrong. Frankly I doubt Kasper, a thoughtful person, would endorse it.

I like Jody Kasper and hold her in high regard. She and I have a good, positive respectful relationship, and this proposal aside, I'm happy she's the police chief. But as I told her at the first public meeting at the Northampton Senior Center about this proposal, "I think, this is the worst idea you've ever had."

I stand by that comment—and make one more.

The chief's response to me that evening was funny! She said, "Well probably actually not my worst idea ever."

Game on! So I added—all this is happening before a crowd of perhaps 150 people at the Senior Center—"Well the worst one you've ever shared with me." And she said, "Well, that's probably true."

As this good-natured exchange tends to show, we live in quite an extraordinary town. For me, not being under constant government surveillance when downtown is an important part of the beauty and fabric of Northampton.

I hope the City Council will expeditiously consider and pass its surveillance nonproliferation ordinance, which is critically important to preserving the city we love.

## EVALUATING THE AUTHOR'S ARGUMENTS:

Viewpoint author Bill Newman argues that surveillance cameras should not be installed in the city. What does his reference to George Orwell mean as he uses it to refer to city officials? What might be the author's intention in using this reference?

# Integrity Could Improve the Surveillance Society

**Steve Mann and Joshua Gans**

*"Being watched feels creepy, but if surveillance is in a public place, others are being watched too, with potential safety benefits for all of us."*

In the following viewpoint, Steve Mann and Joshua Gans argue that surveillance is common in today's society. They suggest that many people would approve of surveillance if it was done with permission instead of under secrecy. The authors argue that a state of integrity should and must be applied to the surveillance industry and be used by any surveillant, whether it is a shopkeeper, the police, or the government. Steve Mann is a professor of strategic management at the University of Toronto. Joshua Gans is a professor of electrical and computer engineering at the University of Toronto.

AS YOU READ, CONSIDER THE FOLLOWING QUESTIONS:
  1. Does anyone see the value of surveillance, according to the authors?
  2. What two important actions could make surveillance better?
  3. What action by ordinary individuals can complicate the results of surveillance technology?

At this moment, there are likely many eyes on you. If you are reading this article in a public place, a surveillance camera might be capturing your actions and even watching you enter your login information and password. Suffice it to say, being watched is part of life today.

Our governments and industry leaders hide their cameras inside domes of wine-dark opacity so we can't see which way the camera is looking, or even if there is a camera in the dome at all. They're shrouded in secrecy. But who is watching them and ensuring the data they collect as evidence against us is reliable?

## You Are Being Watched

We all have varying opinions on how we feel about this pervasive surveillance. Being watched feels creepy, but if surveillance is in a public place, others are being watched too, with potential safety benefits for all of us. We are often watched by lifeguards at a beach or pool, and the benefits are often comforting. So, while it may be easy to claim you don't like being watched, it is sometimes the case that you actually want someone watching over you.

Permission plays an important role in our attitudes about being watched. We don't mind being watched if we have given our consent to do so. But many public surveillance cameras are being used without our consent. And other individuals might just start recording us without our permission. Moreover, individual police as well as police forces in North America are being equipped with body worn cameras. Police and citizens alike have often spoke out in favor of this practice.

But who will it really protect? Will the video only be available in situations where it supports the officer's side of the story? Will the

*Surveillance might be more palatable if it weren't so one-sided. As it is, the surveillant holds all the power.*

camera be said to have mysteriously malfunctioned when the video would have supported a suspect's side of the story? Is there not a conflict-of-interest inherent in one party being the curators of the recordings they make of highly contested disputes with other parties?

Surveillance has become a "one-way mirror." We're being watched but can't watch back.

## A Loss of Integrity
Our contention is that the key word missing from most discussions of surveillance is "integrity." To understand this contention, it is useful to think of its opposite: hypocrisy. In many establishments there is often a surveillance camera pointed at you, while, at the same time, you are prohibited from using your own camera. We see this, for example, at shopping malls, stores, and even in allegedly public spaces.

Store owners are recording your actions so they have evidence if they accuse you of doing something wrong, such as shoplifting. But if you catch them doing something wrong, like having their fire exits illegally chained shut, or if you simply want to prove your innocence from their allegations of wrongdoing, you might want to record them. If there is a dispute, the two recordings might make it more difficult for either party to falsify their recording.

A plausible reason that a surveillant—be it a shopkeeper, corporation or government—might try to impose a one-sided approach on their surveillance, is the issue of control. If they do something wrong, they can choose to not use or retain their recordings. This one-sided preservation of memory is a serious blow to the surveillance's integrity.

## Who Controls the Camera

Consider the case in July 2005 at the Stockwell subway station in London. The London Metropolitan police shot Jean Charles de Menezes seven times in the head with hollow-point bullets, rendering his body "unrecognizable." Hollow-point bullets are used by law enforcement but illegal in war. It turned out the police shot the wrong person (he looked similar to a suspect they were looking for). It was a case of mistaken identity. After the shooting, the police seized the four recordings of the event and reported that all were blank, even though transit officials had already viewed the shooting.

The same issue is at play in any form of surveillance: the surveillants have control over their recordings, and if these are the only ones, the one-sided curation of the evidence undermines their integrity.

How can we resolve this problem of integrity in surveillance? Some solutions are taking effect as we speak, while others will require a gradual change in laws or public attitudes. And some will even create new economic and business opportunities in new markets for integrity-based solutions.

## The Recorded Becoming the Recorder

The increase in so-called cyborg technologies—in which a person's sight or memory disability is augmented with a wearable computer vision system—may help resolve the problem of one-sided surveillants falsifying their recordings. A storeowner may not legally deny entry to a person with such a device, and that recording or a logfile of it could become evidence that the store's own recording of an incident was tampered with. Failing eyesight and memory among our aging population, along with technological breakthroughs, mean that we're going to see more and more instances of people with wearable or implantable cameras to help them see and remember better.

Similarly, the growing prevalence of smartphones and wearable computers with cameras means we're entering an era of inverse surveillance in which, by sheer number, people are likely to record events even if there is a rule against recording. For example, police brutality is often captured by a large number of individuals from different recording angles. Even when police try and prohibit or destroy the recordings, it is difficult for them to guarantee that all the recordings have been destroyed, especially in the age of wireless communications and live transmission.

## A Better Surveillance Bureau

Beyond that, we propose a whole new model or alliance (which we call the "Priveillance Institute") to resolve the lack of integrity in our surveillance society. That is, to force the surveillants (such as shopkeepers or corporations) to bear a cost if they forbid the rest of us from recording them in return.

A "Veillance Contract," for example, would deny the surveillant the right to use its recordings as evidence if it doesn't allow others the right to make their own recordings. Or if the surveillant destroys anyone's tapes or files of an incident. By prohibiting others from recording, the surveillant increases the economic cost for a court to determine what actually happened, thus making justice more expensive to administer.

Another way to promote surveillance integrity would be to do something analogous to the way media businesses use crowdsourcing to rate everything from doctors to taxi drivers. Along these lines we propose creating a third-party validation of surveillance recordings.

In a way that is analogous to the Better Business Bureau, participating organizations could have their surveillance streamed in real time to a trusted, third-party group for verification, which we dub "Videscrow" or Video Escrow—thus reducing their ability to falsify or deny the existence of the recordings. Confidentiality could be built into the system as needed, and these organizations—be they shopkeepers or police departments—would be allowed to display a logo certifying their participation in Videscrow. Establishments with potentially corrupt surveillance would be listed in a database as such until they retracted their no recording policies or submitted to third-party verification such as Videscrow.

These suggestions serve as a good starting place to ensure integrity becomes an integral part of surveillance so that recordings can be trusted as evidence and not be under the exclusive control of one party. There are many paths to doing this, all of which lead to other options and issues that need to be considered. But unless we start establishing principles on these matters, we will be perpetuating a lack of integrity regarding surveillance technologies and their uses.

## EVALUATING THE AUTHORS' ARGUMENTS:

Viewpoint authors Steve Mann and Joshua Gans maintain that integrity plays a large part in today's surveillance society. What does integrity mean? Define the term and explain why integrity might be important to the subject of surveillance in the United States.

# Chapter 3

# Does High-Level Surveillance Threaten Americans' Liberty?

*Is the NSA's aggressive surveillance program an example of government overreach?*

# Surveillance Helps the NSA Spy on Americans

*"The National Security Agency has been intercepting Americans' phone calls and Internet communications."*

**Electronic Frontier Foundation**

In the following viewpoint, the Electronic Frontier Foundation (EFF) argues that the US government has been conducting illegal surveillance on Americans for quite a while. The author maintains that telecommunications companies are assisting the government in these surveillance programs. EFF reports on the actions of their organization to regain and secure the privacy rights of Americans. The Electronic Frontier Foundation works to safeguard civil liberties in the digital world.

**AS YOU READ, CONSIDER THE FOLLOWING QUESTIONS:**
1. For how long has supposed illegal government surveillance gone on?
2. How does EFF fight charges of illegal surveillance, as reported in the viewpoint?
3. What is the occupation of the individual American who has challenged the data collecting scheme of the government?

T he US government, with assistance from major telecommunications carriers including AT&T, has engaged in massive, illegal dragnet surveillance of the domestic communications and communications records of millions of ordinary Americans since at least 2001. Since this was first reported on by the press and discovered by the public in late 2005, EFF has been at the forefront of the effort to stop it and bring government surveillance programs back within the law and the Constitution.

News reports in December 2005 first revealed that the National Security Agency (NSA) has been intercepting Americans' phone calls and Internet communications. Those news reports, combined with a *USA Today* story in May 2006 and the statements of several members of Congress, revealed that the NSA is also receiving wholesale copies of Americans' telephone and other communications records. All of these surveillance activities are in violation of the privacy safeguards established by Congress and the US Constitution.

In early 2006, EFF obtained whistleblower evidence from former AT&T technician Mark Klein showing that AT&T is cooperating with the illegal surveillance. The undisputed documents show that AT&T installed a fiber optic splitter at its facility at 611 Folsom Street in San Francisco that makes copies of all emails, web browsing and other Internet traffic to and from AT&T customers and provides those copies to the NSA. This copying includes both domestic and international Internet activities of AT&T customers. As one expert observed, "this isn't a wiretap, it's a country-tap."

Secret government documents, published by the media in 2013, confirm the NSA obtains full copies of everything that is carried along major domestic fiber optic cable networks. In June 2013, the media, led by the *Guardian* and *Washington Post,* started publishing a series of articles, along with full government documents, that have confirmed much of what was reported in 2005 and 2006 and then some. The reports showed—and the government later admitted—that the government is mass collecting phone metadata of all US customers under the guise of the Patriot Act. Moreover, the media reports confirm that the government is collecting and analyzing the content of communications of foreigners talking to persons inside the United States, as well as collecting much more, without a probable cause

*While most of us are not likely to be on the NSA's radar, the government does collect records and data from Americans' phone use.*

warrant. Finally, the media reports confirm the "upstream" collection off of the fiber optic cables that Mr. Klein first revealed in 2006.

## EFF Fights Back in the Courts

EFF is fighting these illegal activities in the courts. Currently, EFF is representing victims of the illegal surveillance program in *Jewel v. NSA*, a lawsuit filed in September 2008 seeking to stop the warrantless wiretapping and hold the government and government officials behind the program accountable. In July 2013, a federal judge ruled that the government could not rely on the controversial "state secrets" privilege to block our challenge to the constitutionality of the program. On February 10, 2015, however, the court granted summary judgment to the government on the Plaintiffs' allegations of Fourth Amendment violations based on the NSA's copying of Internet traffic from the Internet backbone. The court ruled that the publicly available information did not paint a complete picture of how the NSA collects Internet traffic, so the court could not rule on the program without looking at information that could constitute "state secrets." The court did

not rule that the NSA's activities are legal, nor did it rule on the other claims in *Jewel*, and the case will go forward on those claims. This case is being heard in conjunction with *Shubert v. Obama*, which raises similar claims.

In July 2013, EFF filed another lawsuit, *First Unitarian v. NSA*, based on the recently published FISA court order demanding Verizon turn over all customer phone records including who is talking to whom, when and for how long—to the NSA. This so-called "metadata," especially when collected in bulk and aggregated, allows the government to track the associations of various political and religious organizations. The Director of National Intelligence has since confirmed that the collection of Verizon call records is part of a broader program.

In addition to making the same arguments we made in *Jewel*, we argue in *First Unitarian* that this type of collection violates the First Amendment right to association. Previously, in *Hepting v. AT&T*, EFF filed the first case against a cooperating telecom for violating its customers' privacy. After Congress expressly intervened and passed the FISA Amendments Act to allow the Executive to require dismissal of the case, *Hepting* was ultimately dismissed by the US Supreme Court.

In September of 2014, EFF, along with the American Civil Liberties Union (ACLU) and the American Civil Liberties Union of Idaho, joined the legal team for Anna Smith, an Idaho emergency neonatal nurse, in her challenge of the government's bulk collection of the telephone records of millions of innocent Americans. In

*Smith v. Obama*, we are arguing the program violated her Fourth Amendment rights by collecting a wealth of detail about her familial, political, professional, religious and intimate associations. In particular, we focus on challenging the applicability of the so-called "third party doctrine," the idea that people have no expectation of privacy in information they entrust to others.

## EVALUATING THE AUTHOR'S ARGUMENTS:

In this viewpoint, the Electronic Frontier Foundation argues that the US government is spying on American citizens through the telecommunication systems. Do you believe this accusation? How might this revelation change the way you communicate on your cellphone?

*"Americans were almost equally divided in a 2014 survey over whether the [Snowden] leaks had served or harmed the public interest."*

# American Attitudes About Privacy Are Conflicted and Divided

**Pew Research Center**

In the following viewpoint, the Pew Research Center presents a report centered around the beliefs of the American public when it comes to the issue of surveillance. Much of the data contained in the survey centers around the time after Edward Snowden leaked damning evidence that pointed to government-led surveillance. The Pew Research Center is an American think tank that informs the public about issues important to the world.

**AS YOU READ, CONSIDER THE FOLLOWING QUESTIONS:**
1. According to this viewpoint, do Americans favor anti-terrorist or civil liberty programs?
2. What is the most sensitive piece of personal information?
3. What did most people surveyed say could help privacy issues?

"The State of Privacy in Post-Snowden America," Pew Research Center, September 21, 2016. Reprinted by permission.

After the June 2013 leaks by government contractor Edward Snowden about National Security Agency surveillance of Americans' online and phone communications, Pew Research Center began an in-depth exploration of people's views and behaviors related to privacy. Our report earlier this year about how Americans think about privacy and sharing personal information was a capstone of this two-and-a-half-year effort that examined how people viewed not only government surveillance but also commercial transactions involving the capture of personal information.

Soon after the Snowden leaks surfaced, Americans were almost equally divided in a 2014 survey over whether the leaks had served or harmed the public interest. And, at that time, a majority of Americans believed Snowden should be prosecuted. (A campaign, led by the American Civil Liberties Union, has since been organized to seek a pardon for him.)

However much the Snowden revelations may have contributed to the debate over privacy versus anti-terrorism efforts, Americans today—after a series of terrorist events at home and abroad—are more concerned that anti-terrorist programs don't go far enough than they are about restrictions on civil liberties. An August-September survey found that Americans held that view by a 49% to 33% margin.

In this digital age, Americans' awareness and concerns over issues of privacy also extend beyond the kinds of surveillance programs revealed by Snowden and include how their information is treated by companies with which they do business. Our research also has explored that subject in depth. Here are some of the important findings that emerged from this work:

# 1.

Overall, Americans are divided when it comes to their level of concern about surveillance programs. In a survey conducted November 2014–January 2015, 52% described themselves as "very concerned" or "somewhat concerned" about government surveillance of Americans' data and electronic communications, compared with 46% who described themselves as "not very concerned" or "not at all concerned" about the surveillance. Those who followed the news

*Technology can enhance our lives, but it also makes us vulnerable to breaches of privacy and security.*

about the Snowden leaks and the ensuing debates were more anxious about privacy policy and their own privacy than those who did not.

The public generally believes it is acceptable for the government to monitor many others, including foreign citizens, foreign leaders and American leaders. Yet 57% said it was *unacceptable* for the government to monitor the communications of US citizens. At the same time, majorities supported monitoring of those particular individuals who use words like "explosives" and "automatic weapons" in their search engine queries (65% said that) and those who visit anti-American websites (67% said that).

## 2.

Some 86% of internet users have taken steps online to remove or mask their digital footprints, but many say they would like to do more or are unaware of tools they could use. The actions that users *have* taken range from clearing cookies to encrypting their email, from avoiding using their name to using virtual networks that mask their internet protocol (IP) address. And 55% of internet users have taken steps to avoid observation by specific people, organizations or the government. Many say the purpose of their attempted anonymity is to avoid "social surveillance" by friends and colleagues, rather than the government or law enforcement.

At the same time, many express a desire to take additional steps to protect their data online. When asked if they feel as though their own efforts to protect the privacy of their personal information online are sufficient, 61% say they feel they "would like to do more," while 37% say they "already do enough." Even after news broke about the NSA surveillance programs, few Americans took sophisticated steps to protect their data, and many were unaware of robust actions they could take to hide their online activities. Some 34% of those who said they were aware of the NSA surveillance programs in a July 2013 survey (30% of all adults) had taken at least one step to hide or shield their information from the government. But most of those actions were simple steps, such as changing their privacy settings on social media or avoiding certain apps, rather than tools like email encryption programs, "don't track" plug-ins for browsers or anonymity software.

## 3.

Americans express a consistent lack of confidence about the security of everyday communication channels and the organizations that control them—particularly when it comes to the use of online tools. And they exhibited a deep lack of faith in organizations of all kinds, public or private, in protecting the personal information they collect. Only tiny minorities say they are "very confident" that the records maintained by these organizations will remain private and secure.

## 4.

Some 74% say it is "very important" to them that they be in control of who can get information about them, and 65% say it is "very important" to them to control what information is collected about them. Personal control matters a lot to people. If the traditional American view of privacy is the "right to be left alone," the 21st-century refinement of that idea is the right to control their identity and information. They understand that modern life won't allow them to be "left alone" and untracked, but they do want to have a say in how their personal information is used.

## 5.

Many Americans struggle to understand the nature and scope of data collected about them. When it comes to their own role in managing their personal information, most adults are not sure what information is being collected or how it is being used.

While half of those surveyed said they felt confident they understood how their information would be used, 47% said they were not, and many of these people felt confused, discouraged or impatient when trying to make decisions about sharing their personal information with companies.

## 6.

Fully 91% of adults agree or strongly agree that consumers have lost control of how personal information is collected and used by companies. Half of internet users said they worry about the amount of information available about them online, and most said they knew about key pieces of their personal information that could be found on the internet. Only 9% say they feel they have "a lot" of control over how much information is collected about them and how it is used. Indeed, experts we canvassed about the future of privacy argued that privacy was no longer a "condition" of American life. Rather, they asserted that it was becoming a commodity to be purchased.

## 7.

For most Americans who are making decisions about sharing their information in return for a product, service or other benefit, the context and conditions of the transactions matter. When considering this basic digital era trade-off, many are in an "It depends" frame of mind. Risk-benefit calculations that enter people's minds during the decision process include the terms of the deal; the circumstances of their lives; whether they consider the company or organization involved to be trustworthy; what happens to their data after they are collected, especially if the data are made available to third parties; and how long the data will be retained.

For instance, 54% of Americans consider it an acceptable trade-off to have surveillance cameras in the office in order to improve workplace security and help reduce thefts. But a scenario involving the use of a "smart thermostat" in people's homes that might save energy costs in return for insight about people's comings and goings was deemed "acceptable" by only 27% of adults. It was seen as "not acceptable" by 55%.

Indeed, most Americans assign different degrees of value to different pieces of information. Social Security numbers are ranked as the most sensitive information, while people's purchasing habits ranked lowest as something they felt was very sensitive.

## 8.

Young adults generally are more focused than their elders when it comes to online privacy. Younger adults are more likely to know that personal information about them is available online and to have experienced privacy problems. By the same token, our surveys have found that those ages 18 to 29 are more likely than older adults to say they have paid attention to privacy issues, tried to protect their privacy and reported some kind of harm because of privacy problems. They are more likely to have limited the amount of personal information available about them online, changed privacy settings, deleted unwanted comments on social media, removed their name from photos in which they were tagged, and taken steps to mask their identities while online. It is also true that younger adults are more likely to have shared personal information online.

## 9.

A majority of the US public believes changes in law could make a difference in protecting privacy—especially when it comes to policies on retention of their data. In the midst of all this uncertainty and angst about privacy, Americans are generally in favor of additional legal protections against abuses of their data. Some 68% of internet users believe current laws are not good enough in protecting people's privacy online; and 64% believe the government should do more to regulate advertisers. Most expect at least some limits on retention policies by data collections. And a majority (64%) support more regulation of advertisers and the way they handle personal information. When asked about the data the government collects as part of anti-terrorism efforts, 65% of Americans say there are not adequate limits on "what telephone and internet data the government can collect."

## 10.

Many technology experts predict that few individuals will have the energy or resources to protect themselves from "dataveillance" in the coming years and that privacy protection will likely become a luxury good. Another prediction from 2,511 experts we canvassed was that the prospect of achieving bygone notions of privacy will become more remote as the Internet of Things takes hold and people's homes, workplaces and the objects around them will "tattle" on them. A more hopeful theme about privacy's future was sounded by experts who argued that new technology tools would become available that would give consumers power to negotiate on equal footing with corporations about information sharing and also allow them to work around governments trying to collect data.

### EVALUATING THE AUTHOR'S ARGUMENTS:

In this viewpoint, Pew Research Center presents statistics showing American attitudes about surveillance by the government. How effective are such statistics in making a case one way or the other about Edward Snowden's actions and about government surveillance in general?

# Privacy Claims Often Clash with the First Amendment

### Judith Haydel

*"In public... there is little or no First Amendment... protection of privacy."*

In the following viewpoint, Judith Haydel provides a detailed analysis of the First Amendment to the Constitution and the rights associated with it. Haydel includes examples of when the First Amendment is and is not clear in regards to privacy issues. The author references court cases that illuminate First Amendment rights. Dr. Judith Haydel was a professor of political science at the University of Louisiana–Lafayette.

**AS YOU READ, CONSIDER THE FOLLOWING QUESTIONS:**

1. Is the right to privacy specifically mentioned in the Constitution?
2. As stated in the viewpoint, where is the First Amendment protection of privacy the greatest?
3. What is complicating the protection of privacy, according to the author?

"The First Amendment Encyclopedia," by Judith Haydel, Middle Tennessee State University. Reprinted by permission.

P rivacy generally refers to an individual's right to seclusion, or right to be free from public interference. Often privacy claims clash with First Amendment rights. For example, individuals may assert a privacy right to be "let alone" when the press reports on their private life or follows them around in an intrusive manner on public and private property.

## Right to Privacy Found in the Constitution

Much like liberty, justice, and democracy, privacy appears to be an easy concept to understand in the abstract. Defining it in a legal context, however, is difficult and complicated by the fact that there are constitutional rights to privacy and also common law or statutory rights of privacy.

There is no explicit mention of privacy in the US Constitution, but in his dissent in *Gilbert v. Minnesota* (1920), Justice Louis D. Brandeis nonetheless stated that the First Amendment protected the privacy of the home. In *Griswold v. Connecticut* (1965), Justice William O. Douglas placed a right to privacy in a "penumbra" cast by the First, Third, Fourth, Fifth, and Ninth Amendments.

## Right to Privacy Found in Common Law

Initially, the common law upon which the US Constitution, state constitutions, and state laws are based protected only property rights. During the 1880s, however, legal scholars began to theorize that the common law of torts, which involves injuries to private persons or property, also protected against government invasion of privacy.

In the late 1880s, Judge Thomas Cooley wrote in *A Treatise on the Law of Torts or the Wrongs Which Arise Independent of Contract* that people had a right to be let alone. Boston lawyers and former Harvard Law School classmates Samuel D. Warren and Louis D. Brandeis elaborated on this concept in their seminal 1890 article in the *Harvard Law Review*, "The Right to Privacy." They argued that the common law's protection of property rights was moving toward the recognition of a right to be let alone. Their article inspired some state courts to begin interpreting the civil law of torts to protect a right of privacy.

*Signed into law in 2001, the USA Patriot Act was meant to tighten national security. But critics charge it ushered in an era of mass surveillance and government overreach.*

## Types of Privacy Claims

Later, Dean William Prosser, a torts law expert, in an influential 1960 article in the *California Law Review* wrote that there are four distinct types of privacy torts:

- intrusion upon solitude,

- public disclosure of private facts,

- appropriation of another's name or image,

- and publishing information that puts a person in a false light.

Sometimes privacy tort claims conflict with First Amendment free speech or free press claims. For example, the press may publish sensitive details of a person's private life and be charged with a public disclosure of private facts tort.

## Supreme Court Has Decided First Amendment Privacy Cases

The Court has rendered a number of decisions involving First Amendment freedoms and privacy. In *Packer Corporation v. Utah* (1932), Justice Brandeis suggested that the Court should consider the conditions under which privacy interests are intruded upon. His suggestion foreshadowed the Court's later development of the distinction between privacy interests in the home and in public.

The First Amendment protection of privacy is greatest when the invasion of privacy occurs in the home or in other places where an individual has a reasonable expectation of privacy. For example, despite the fact that obscenity is not protected by the First Amendment, in *Stanley v. Georgia* (1969) the Court struck down a Georgia law prohibiting the possession of obscene materials in the home. Justice Thurgood Marshall wrote: "If the First Amendment means anything, it means that a State has no business telling a man, sitting alone in his own house, what books he may read or what films he may watch. Our whole constitutional heritage rebels at the thought of giving government the power to control men's minds."

In *Federal Communications Commission v. Pacifica Foundation* (1978), the Court upheld a Federal Communications Commission ban on indecent speech on the radio, because radio broadcasts invade the privacy of the home, it is difficult to avoid them, and children have access to them.

## Little First Amendment Protection of Privacy in Public

In public, on the other hand, there is little or no First Amendment protection of privacy. In *Cohen v. California* (1971), the Court held that the privacy concerns of individuals in a public place were outweighed by the First Amendment's protection of speech, even when the speech included profanity in a political statement written on a man's jacket.

# Fast Fact

The First Amendment was originally passed by Congress on September 25, 1789, and later ratified in 1791.

## Freedom of Association Is Strongest First Amendment Protection for Privacy

Court decisions involving privacy rights are sometimes based on more than one First Amendment provision, and it can be difficult to differentiate privacy cases on the basis of a specific First Amendment right. In general, the strongest First Amendment protection for privacy is in the right of freedom of assembly and, by judicial interpretation, freedom of association. That protection, however, is not absolute: organizations whose goals are unlawful are not protected.

In *De Jonge v. Oregon* (1937), the Court declared that the right of people peaceably to assemble does not extend to associations that incite violence or crime. The Court in *NAACP v. Alabama* (1958) ruled that freedom of assembly includes the right to freedom of association and acknowledged that individuals are free to associate for the collective advocacy of ideas. Compelled disclosure of the NAACP's membership lists, which was at issue in the case, would in effect suppress the Association's ability to do business and hinder the group's members from expressing their views.

## Privacy Rights Usually Take Back Seat to Media Rights

Although the press does not have additional First Amendment rights that the public does not also enjoy, privacy rights ordinarily take a back seat to the media's right to gather and publish truthful information that is available in public documents. For example, in *Cox Broadcasting Corp. v. Cohn* (1975), the Court ruled that freedom of the press interests in publishing publicly available information about the commission of a crime outweighed privacy rights. And in *Bartnicki v. Vopper* (2001), the Court upheld the right of a radio station to broadcast a private telephone conversation involving public persons and concerning political matters that was illegally intercepted by an anonymous third party.

## Technology Advances and National Security Interests Are Making Privacy Rights More Complex

Advances in technology, including the ubiquity of the Internet, are far outpacing government's ability to address privacy issues in these new and ever-changing contexts. To make matters even more complex, national security interests are now entangled in this web of technological sophistication.

National security concerns in the wake of the September 11, 2001, destruction of the World Trade Center led to passage of the USA Patriot Act. Parts of the act expand government power to conduct surveillance of Americans. Although it prohibits investigations of Americans' activities that are protected by the First Amendment, some government actions have been challenged in the courts as violating First Amendment rights. Early cases involved the National Security Agency's wiretapping practices and a gag order provision that prevented recipients of national security letters from revealing they had received such a letter. It will take future litigation to determine the proper balance between privacy and national security.

## EVALUATING THE AUTHOR'S ARGUMENTS:

In this viewpoint, Judith Haydel presents a balanced argument concerning the First Amendment and privacy rights. If the Founding Fathers were alive today, how might they respond to the challenges of privacy rights since 9/11?

# The Public Deserves Surveillance Transparency

**Dave Maass**

> *"Who should decide which surveillance technologies are appropriate for our communities?"*

In the following viewpoint, Dave Maass analyzes the issue of high-tech surveillance equipment used by police in California. He cites the importance of privacy as an inalienable right in that state. The author contends that there must be trust between communities and the public they govern. Dave Maass is a senior investigative researcher at the Electronic Frontier Foundation.

**AS YOU READ, CONSIDER THE FOLLOWING QUESTIONS:**

1. What population is being targeted for surveillance, according to the author?
2. According to the author, have any California communities passed laws limiting the use of surveillance equipment?
3. What are two reasons the government might use to explain its use of high-tech surveillance as noted in this viewpoint?

Commentary: Public in Urgent Need of Surveillance Transparency," by Dave Maass, *The San Diego Union-Tribune*, May 27, 2017. https://www.sandiegouniontribune.com/opinion/commentary/sd-utbg -surveillance-transparency-privacy-20170526-story.html. Licensed under CC By 3.0 US.

In 2015, a local resident joined a nationwide project to uncover how police use face recognition devices. He filed a public records request with the Carlsbad Police Department, which quickly responded that no documents existed because the city didn't use that technology.

This was demonstrably false: Carlsbad police had been part of a regional face recognition pilot program for years. Eventually, CPD admitted 14 officers carried special smartphones that capture faces and match them against the county's mug shot database.

But Carlsbad could not produce policies, protocols or guidelines for how officers may operate the devices. Nor did the city know how many times the devices were used.

Surveillance technology is rapidly advancing and can consist of automated license plate readers that track our travel patterns, fake cell towers that surreptitiously connect to our smartphones, algorithms that scrape our social media or devices that digitize our faces. Many technologies aren't limited to gathering intelligence on suspects and instead collect information on everyone.

The Carlsbad incident raises questions about public trust and high-tech policing. Who should decide which surveillance technologies are appropriate for our communities? Should police have to disclose how these technologies are used and how often they're abused?

Privacy and public safety are not mutually exclusive; it just takes a robust debate to land on the right balance. This conversation won't happen unless the rules change so police obtain approval from the public and our elected officials prior to deploying invasive spy tech.

A bill before the California legislature—Senate Bill 21—would ensure that police do not acquire surveillance technology without a public process.

Before moving forward, a law enforcement agency would submit a usage policy for public review during an open meeting. Elected representatives (e.g. a city council) would have the authority to approve or reject the technology. In exigent circumstances, police could temporarily bypass the process, but they would need to stop using such surveillance technology and submit proper disclosures after the emergency has passed.

*A US surveillance camera overlooks the international bridge between Mexico and the United States.*

Police and sheriff departments would publish biennial transparency reports, disclosing the kinds of data the technologies collect, how many times each technology was deployed, how often each technology helped catch a suspect or close a case, and the number of times the systems were misused.

In 1972, Californians voted to include privacy as an inalienable right in the state's Constitution. "The proliferation of government snooping and data collecting is threatening to destroy our traditional freedoms," the amendment's authors wrote. They warned technology would allow police to create "cradle-to-grave" profiles of every American, which then could be used to humiliate us.

One need only look to nearby Calexico. In 2014, police spent nearly $100,000 from a slush fund of seized assets on sophisticated spy gear. They then allegedly used these systems to run illegal surveillance on city council members with the intent to extort. A US Department of Justice investigation confirmed this corruption—but also found a troubling pattern in which the city approved a network of surveillance cameras, body cameras and automated license plate reader technology "before implementing the essential fundamentals of policing."

To head off these kinds of threats to privacy, Santa Clara County has already passed an ordinance promoting transparency about surveillance technology. Other cities are considering similar measures.

SB 21, a bill by Sen. Jerry Hill, D-San Mateo, would implement statewide standards—an important step for San Diego County, where police technology often flows freely between agencies. The bill enhances fiscal responsibility by providing policymakers with data to evaluate whether a costly technology is as effective as vendors claim.

As the US government ramps up a new "War on Drugs" and aggressive immigration enforcement, we anticipate even more military-grade surveillance technology to flow down to local agencies through grant programs, equipment transfers and federal partnerships. California lawmakers must pass SB 21 to put adequate controls in place so these technologies are operated responsibly, transparently and with respect for our constitutional rights.

## EVALUATING THE AUTHOR'S ARGUMENTS:

Viewpoint author Dave Maass argues that police should not automatically be able to institute high-tech spy equipment without the consent of the community or elected officials. Do you agree? Why or why not? Which specific arguments brought you to this conclusion?

# Facial Recognition Technology Can Be Used for Good Reason

*"26 US states permit law enforcement to query the photos and information contained on driver's licenses."*

**Marcia Wendorf**

In the following viewpoint, Marcia Wendorf argues that facial recognition technology has a positive side and provides examples to support her opinion. The author provides details about several countries where this technology is already in use, as well as places in the United States that currently deploy facial recognition software. Marcia Wendorf writes about the latest developments in science, medical issues, and governmental policy.

**AS YOU READ, CONSIDER THE FOLLOWING QUESTIONS:**
1. Is facial recognition technology accurate, according to the author?
2. From the statistics in the viewpoint, which country has a large number of missing children?
3. Which large US company uses facial recognition technology?

"Facial Recognition Technology Is Being Used to Find Missing Children," by Marcia Wendorf, Interesting Engineering, Inc., December 20, 2019. Reprinted by permission.

I t's every parent's worst nightmare: their child goes missing. In 2009, three-year-old Gui Hao went missing from his family's wine shop in Guang'an City in Sichuan Province, China.

In December 2017, a facial recognition system created by Youtu Lab, a division of Tencent, was introduced into the Sichuan Provincial Public Security Department. The system uses artificial intelligence (AI) to detect gender and age in photographs.

Experts within the Sichuan police adopted an innovative approach: they used machines to teach other machines, training a neural network to recognize human faces, regardless of age, to an accuracy of greater than 96%.

In 2019, using the new technology, authorities found Gui Hao in Guangdong Province and reunited him with his family.

In April 2018, police in New Delhi, India, began using a new facial recognition system to search for the incredibly high number of missing children in that city, 45,000. In all of India, almost 200,000 children are missing.

The new facial recognition system uses machine learning to identify similarities in faces seen on different pictures. Since its inauguration, police have found 2,930 of the missing children.

## Amazon's Rekognition

Amazon's new facial recognition system, Rekognition, is being used by police in Orlando, Florida, to search through footage from the city's many video surveillance cameras.

Washington County, Oregon, has built a Rekognition-based mobile app that is being used by its police. Officers can submit an image to the county's database of 300,000 faces, and the system will search for a match.

According to a Huffington Post article, Rekognition can identify "all faces in group photos, crowded events, and public places such as airports." It is also capable of recognizing up to 100 people in a single picture.

In May 2018, the American Civil Liberties Union (ACLU) sent an open letter to Amazon's CEO Jeff Bezos, asking him to stop Amazon's contributions to government surveillance. The letter included this: "Local police could use it [Rekognition] to identify political protesters

*Facial recognition technology has been effective in finding missing children. But many people are concerned the technology will be used for less noble purposes.*

captured by officer body cameras. With Rekognition, Amazon delivers these dangerous surveillance powers directly to the government."

A 2016 study by Georgetown University's Law Center on Privacy and Technology found that the faces of more than 117 million Americans are already included in government facial recognition databases that are used by law enforcement.

The study found that the faces of half of all US adults are in such databases and that 25% of state and local law enforcement agencies are already running facial recognition searches.

Even more troubling, the study found a lack of oversight on the use of photo databases, and that 26 US states permit law enforcement to query the photos and information contained on driver's licenses.

## "Big Brother" in LA?

According to the Stop LAPD Spying Coalition website, police in that city are employing surveillance cameras with highly accurate facial recognition software, license plate readers, drones, police body cameras, and even Stingrays and DRT boxes to spy on its citizens.

Both Stingrays and DRT boxes simulate cell phone towers so that cell phones connect with them rather than the actual towers. The devices can be mounted on aircraft to collect information from cell phones that are believed to be used for criminal activity. The devices can also be used to jam cell phones.

The Stop LAPD Spying Coalition asserts that the LAPD is "crunch[ing] crime statistics and other data with algorithms to 'predict' when and where

future crimes are most likely to occur." If this sounds an awful lot to you like Steven Spielberg's 2002 movie *Minority Report,* starring Tom Cruise, you're not alone.

## Vehicle Recognition

Maryland company Rekor's vehicle recognition software not only recognizes license plates, it also is able to identify a vehicle's make, model, color and year. Since 2017, a quarter of all children who were rescued after being kidnapped was because someone from the public recognized the vehicle involved in the kidnapping.

Robert Lowery of NCMEC [National Center for Missing and Exploited Children] noted that "Rekor's AI will leverage technology to help find those cars even more quickly so we can bring children safely home." Rekor is offering free licenses to law enforcement and other agencies involved with recovering abducted children.

In spite of all these concerns by privacy advocates about facial recognition technology, a spokesperson for India's National Commission for Protection of Child Rights (NCPCR) told the *Independent* newspaper that, "If such a type of software helps trace missing children and reunite them with their families, nothing can be better than this."

## EVALUATING THE AUTHOR'S ARGUMENTS:

Viewpoint author Marcia Wendorf analyzes the potential positive benefits of facial recognition technology.
Construct a table showing the positive and negative results of this technology using details from the viewpoint.

# Americans Are Fighting Their Governments Over Facial Recognition Surveillance

*"The FBI has done little in the last three years to make sure that its search results are accurate."*

**Nathan Sheard**

In the following viewpoint, Nathan Sheard argues that facial recognition surveillance should be stopped. Sheard details the steps that some US states are already taking toward this goal, while some have already outlawed the technology. In conclusion, Sheard suggests that vendors of this equipment are one of the most outspoken groups supporting the technology. Nathan Sheard is the associate director of community organizing for the Electronic Frontier Foundation.

**AS YOU READ, CONSIDER THE FOLLOWING QUESTIONS:**

1. Which two US states have laws against facial recognition surveillance, according to the viewpoint?
2. Which three US Constitutional Amendments and their promised rights are threatened by facial recognition surveillance?
3. Who is against the regulation of facial recognition surveillance?

Vendors woo law enforcement with a seemingly inexhaustible flow of new spy tech. This places concerned community members, civil society, and lawmakers in a seemingly Sisyphean struggle of trying to keep up with new technological threats to privacy, and to shepherd the adoption of enforceable policy to protect essential civil liberties. If 2018 was the year of communities standing together in the fight for democratic control over whether or not police may acquire surveillance technology, 2019 was the year that many of these same communities led the charge to ban government face surveillance.

## Local Bans

In May of this year, San Francisco became the first city in the United States to ban local government use of face surveillance technology. San Francisco's ban was enacted with overwhelming support from the City's Board of Supervisors as part of the city's Stop Secret Surveillance Ordinance. The Stop Secret Surveillance Ordinance banned the use of face surveillance by local government. It also provided the Community Control of Police Surveillance (CCOPS) protections that had already been adopted in neighboring Oakland and Berkeley—and close to a dozen other cities nationwide. By October, Berkeley and Oakland followed suit, amending their existing CCOPS laws to include outright bans on their own city agencies using face surveillance technology.

The Bay Area was not alone in proactively protecting residents from this particularly pernicious form of surveillance. Just weeks before Oakland's City Council voted unanimously in support of banning the technology, the Metro-Boston community of Somerville, Massachusetts, passed its own standalone ban. With a similarly unanimous vote, Somerville became the second city in the nation to enact a ban, and the first East Coast city to do so. Before the end of 2019, Somerville would be joined by the nearby town of Brookline. Should a ban currently under consideration in Cambridge, MA, pass, the Boston area could closely mirror the Bay Area's trifecta of protected communities. Meanwhile, legislators in both Portland, Maine, and Portland, Oregon (the largest cities in these two states) have introduced bills looking to ban their own local agencies from using face surveillance.

*Concerns have arisen that protesters, such as those who took to the street to support the Black Lives Matter movement in 2020, could end up in facial recognition databases.*

In a sign of intensifying battles ahead, November saw Microsoft dispatch representatives to challenge Portland, ME's proposed ban. Also in November, EFF launched our About Face campaign. Organized in collaboration with community-based organizations in the Electronic Frontier Alliance—and other concerned civil society organizations—our About Face campaign aids residents in communities throughout the United States in calling for an end to government use of face surveillance.

## State-Level Protections

In early October, California Governor Gavin Newsom signed A.B. 1215 into law. Introduced by State Assembly member Phil Ting, AB 1215 enacts a three-year moratorium on the use of face recognition or other biometric surveillance in combination with police body-cameras—or any similar recording devices carried by law enforcement. While A.B. 1215 officially goes into effect on January 1, 2020, the law is already credited with the planned suspension of San Diego's Tactical Identification System (TACIDS) program—one of the largest, longest-running, and most controversial face recognition programs operated by local law enforcement in the United States. Lawmakers in New York State are considering legislation similar to California's A.B. 1215, while less protective alternatives are being considered in Washington State and Michigan.

The Commonwealth of Massachusetts is positioned to go a step further. A pair of Massachusetts bills (S.1385/H.1538) would provide the most robust state-level protections yet: an indefinite moratorium on the use of face surveillance by government agencies within the commonwealth, until such time as the state legislature enacts an authorizing statute. Such a law would have to clearly outline what agencies are permitted to use the technology, require audits, protect civil liberties, and establish minimum accuracy rates to prevent disparate impact against women, people with darker skin, and young people.

## What About the Feds?

There are currently no federal regulations regarding the use of face surveillance technology. During hearings held by the House Committee on Oversight and Reform, a bipartisan group of representatives including Rep. Alexandria Ocasio-Cortez (D-NY), as well as ranking member Rep. Jim Jordan (R-OH), said they intend to draft legislation addressing face surveillance. This legislation has yet to materialize. The continued failure of federal elected officials to address the threat that face surveillance poses to rights promised in the First, Fourth, and Fourteenth Amendments only serves to underscore the importance of local and state-level bans and moratoria.

In June, the US Government Accountability Office (GAO) issued an update to its 2016 report on the FBI's use of face recognition. As EFF's Surveillance Litigation Director Jen Lynch explained, it's still terrible. Although GAO criticized the FBI in 2016 for failing to conduct accuracy assessments of its Next Generation Identification (NGI) database, or the searches it performs on its state and federal partners' databases, the FBI has done little in the last three years to make sure that its search results are accurate.

According to the report, the FBI also neglected to determine whether the face recognition systems of its external partners—states and other federal agencies—are sufficiently accurate to prevent innocent people from being wrongly identified as criminal suspects. While the FBI claims that it has no authority to set or enforce accuracy standards outside the agency, the GAO disagreed, given that the FBI is using these external databases as a component of its routine operations.

The original GAO report heavily criticized the FBI for rolling out these massive face recognition capabilities without ever explaining the privacy implications of its actions to the public. The current report reiterates those concerns.

## The Road Ahead

These battles undoubtedly will continue on the state, local, and federal levels. We can expect that surveillance vendors and law enforcement agencies will continue to oppose legislation intended to protect the public from face surveillance and other forms of privacy-invasive surveillance technology. At the same time, communities across the US will continue to band together to protect themselves from the harms of the ever-expanding panopticon of unwarranted government surveillance. Through efforts like our About Face campaign, and alongside our EFA allies—and other civil society partners—we will continue the push for stronger, enforceable protections. If your community-based group or hackerspace would like to join us in bringing an end to government use of face surveillance, please add your names to the About Face petition and join the Alliance.

**EVALUATING THE AUTHOR'S ARGUMENTS:**

Viewpoint author Nathan Sheard maintains that the practice of facial recognition surveillance should stop. Do you agree or disagree? Construct an argument for your position using details from this viewpoint and the previous viewpoints.

# Facts About the Surveillance State

Editor's note: These facts can be used in reports to add credibility when making important points or claims.

## Important Dates Concerning Surveillance

1927—First documented use of surveillance cameras in Russia. A video camera was connected to a television.

1939—Miniature portable cameras appear.

1942—Nazis create a simple CCTV (closed circuit television) system to monitor rocket launches.

1949—The book *Nineteen Eighty-Four* is published. It depicts a surveillance state where police monitor people through devices called telescreens. The term "Big Brother" from the book is still used today to describe government surveillance, as in "Big Brother is watching you."

1950—After 1950, CCTC technology begins to be used in medicine, education, manufacturing, and finance.

1951—The video tape recorder is invented.

1981—President Ronald Reagan signs into law Executive Order 12333, which gives US intelligence services the right to gather intelligence information outside the US.

1990s—Cameras are installed at ATMs to record all transactions.

2001—The USA Patriot Act is signed into law and gives a reason for the government to conduct surveillance.

2002—The Department of Homeland Security (DHS) is made official.

2013—Whistleblower Edward Snowden says the NSA is spying on American citizens.

2014—Facebook says its DeepFace program can identify faces with over 97% accuracy.

2015—The USA Freedom Act updates the Patriot Act.

2018—Amazon markets its facial recognition program Rekognition to law enforcement.

2019—San Francisco, CA, bans the use of facial recognition surveillance (others follow).

## Biometrics

Definition: Biometrics is a secure way of identifying someone by characteristics unique to that individual, such as fingerprints, face, iris scan, and voice.

Common uses: Biometrics are presently used in airports, on smartphones, for banking, and citizen registration (like voting).

## Facial Recognition

Definition: The act of identifying someone by using their face.

Divided into three areas: face detection, face capture, and face match. Face detection locates human faces in video and images. Face capture changes a person's facial features into digital data. Face match verifies information and matches to a certain person.

Identification: Answers the question, "Who are you?"

Verification: Answers the question, "Are you really who you say you are?"

## Important Laws Concerning Surveillance

First Amendment to the US Constitution—Protects free speech.

Fifth Amendment to the US Constitution—Protects against illegal searches.

Foreign Intelligence Surveillance Act (FISA) of 1978—Allowed searches or wiretaps to gather foreign intelligence.

USA Patriot Act—Allowed the US government greater freedom to gather intelligence (spy) on people.

USA Freedom Act—Updated the Patriot Act.

# Organizations to Contact

The editors have compiled the following list of organizations concerned with the issues debated in this book. The descriptions are derived from materials provided by the organizations. All have publications or information available for interested readers. The list was compiled on the date of publication of the present volume; the information provided here may change. Be aware that many organizations take several weeks or longer to respond to inquiries, so allow as much time as possible for the receipt of requested materials.

## American Civil Liberties Union (ACLU)

125 Broad Street, 18th Floor, New York, NY 10004
(212) 549-2500
email: aclupreferences@aclu.org
website: www.aclu.org/
The ACLU is dedicated to maintaining the rights promised by the US Constitution. Its website contains a wealth of information including how to learn about individual rights and how to take action.

## Amnesty International (AI)

5 Penn Plaza, 16th Floor, New York, NY 10001
(212) 807-8400
email: aimember@aiusa.org
website: www.amnesty.org/en/
The Amnesty International organization is a global movement of millions of people. Members work to protect the human rights of people around the globe.

## Brennan Center for Justice (BC)

120 Broadway, Suite 1750, New York, NY 10271
(646) 292-8310
email: brennancenter@nyu.edu
website: www.brennancenter.org/
The Brennan Center for Justice is dedicated to building an America that is just, free, and democratic for everyone.

## CATO Institute

1000 Massachusetts Avenue NW, Washington, DC 20001-5403

(202) 842-0200

website: www.cato.org

CATO Institute is a public policy research organization dedicated to individual freedom, peace, free markets, and limited government.

## Electronic Frontier Foundation (EFF)

815 Eddy Street, San Francisco, CA 94109

(415) 436-9333

email: info@eff.org

website: www.eff.org/about

EFF works to defend civil liberties in the digital world. It is working to keep up with rapidly expanding technological developments.

## Human Rights Watch

350 Fifth Avenue, 34th Floor, New York, NY 10118-3299

(212) 290-4700

website: www.hrw.org/

Human Rights Watch is a globally focused organization that sees its mission as investigating, exposing, and changing abuse happening all over the world.

## National Constitution Center

525 Arch Street, Philadelphia, PA 19106

(215) 409-6600

email: education@constitutioncenter.org

website: constitutioncenter.org

The National Constitution Center disseminates information about the US Constitution.

## National Security Agency (NSA)

9800 Savage Road, Suite 6272, Ft. George G. Meade, MD 20755-6000

(301) 688-6311

website: www.nsa.gov

The NSA works to protect the United States and its citizens. Its priorities include privacy rights, cybersecurity, and cryptology.

# For Further Reading

## Books

Chertoff, Michael. *Exploding Data: Reclaiming Our Cyber Security in the Digital Age.* New York, NY: Atlantic Monthly Press, 2018. Big data is watching you, and the laws and protections set in place years ago need to change and be brought up to date with the explosion of data and information used by business and government.

Edgar, Timothy H. *Beyond Snowden: Privacy, Mass Surveillance, and the Struggle to Reform the NSA.* Washington, DC: Brookings Institution Press, 2017. How can the privacy of Americans be protected with the widespread use of surveillance, especially if it's done in secret? This author argues that transparency must be ensured within the government agencies, especially the NSA.

Ferguson, Andrew G. *The Rise of Big Data Policing: Surveillance, Race, and the Future of Law Enforcement.* New York, NY: New York University Press, 2017. Look inside the world of big data, surveillance cameras, and law enforcement. This book shows how law enforcement has adopted and quite possibly overused surveillance equipment.

Greenwald, Glenn. *No Place to Hide: Edward Snowden, the NSA, and the US Surveillance State.* New York, NY: Henry Holt, 2014. Investigative reporter Greenwald writes about the whistleblower case sparked by Edward Snowden.

Melton, Keith H. *Ultimate Spy.* London, UK: Dorling Kindersley, 2015. This book looks at the inside world of espionage with historical accounts up through the whistleblower Edward Snowden.

Michel, Arthur Holland. *Eyes in the Sky: The Secret Rise of Gorgon Stare and How It Will Watch Us All.* New York, NY: Houghton Mifflin Harcourt, 2019. This book looks at high-tech surveillance equipment from initial use in the military to the present. Learn about Gorgon Stare, the wide area surveillance developed by the US Pentagon.

Rall, Ted. *Snowden.* New York, NY: Seven Stories Press, 2015. This graphic novel explores the life of Edward Snowden, delving into the reasons why he became a whistleblower. It looks at the world of mass surveillance and the technologies that may change the world.

Rogers, Jeni. *200+ Ways to Protect Your Privacy: Simple Ways to Prevent Hacks and Protect Your Privacy—On and Offline.* Avon, MA: Adams Media, 2019. The internet is a great resource but can also cause identify theft and loss of privacy. Learn how to protect your privacy and data with techniques shown in the book.

## Periodicals and Internet Sources

Carlsen, John. "When Did Security Cameras Come Out?" ASecureLife, November 20, 2019. https://www.asecurelife.com/history-of -security-cameras/.

Chokshi, Niraj. "How Surveillance Cameras Could Be Weaponized with A.I.," *New York Times*, June 13, 2019. https://www.nytimes .com/2019/06/13/us/aclu-surveillance-artificial-intelligence.html.

Columbus, Louis. "53% of Companies Are Adopting Big Data Analytics," *Forbes*, December 24, 2017. https://www.forbes.com /sites/louiscolumbus/2017/12/24/53-of-companies-are -adopting-big-data-analytics/#14d046ff39a1.

Crockford, Kade. "The FBI Is Tracking Our Faces in Secret. We're Suing," ACLU, October 31, 2019. https://www.aclu.org/news/privacy -technology/the-fbi-is-tracking-our-faces-in-secret-were-suing/.

Feeney, Matthew. "When It Comes to Surveillance, Watch the Watchmen," Cato Institute, October 23, 2017. https://www.cato.org /publications/commentary/when-it-comes-surveillance-watch -watchmen.

Glanton, Dahleen. "In a City with Tens of Thousands of Surveillance Cameras, Who's Watching Whom?" *Chicago Tribune*, February 26, 2019. https://www.chicagotribune.com/columns/dahleen-glanton/ct-met -dahleen-glanton-video-cameras-chicago-20190225-story.html.

Gorski, Ashley. "The Government Has a Secret Plan to Track Everyone's Faces at Airports. We're Suing," ACLU, March 12, 2020. https://www .aclu.org/news/privacy-technology/the-government-has-a-secret -plan-to-track-everyones-faces-at-airports-were-suing/.

Ilyushina, Mary. "Edward Snowden Requests a Three-Year Extension of Russian Residency," CNN, April 16, 2020. https://www.cnn .com/2020/04/16/europe/edward-snowden-russian-residency -intl/index.html.

Nielsen, Alyssa. "Video Surveillance Threatens Privacy, Experts Say," *Daily Universe*, June 28, 2017. https://universe.byu.edu/2017/06/28/video-surveillance-threatens-privacy/.

Ricker, Thomas. "The US, Like China, Has About One Surveillance Camera for Every Four People, Says Report," The Verge, December 9, 2019. https://www.theverge.com/2019/12/9/21002515/surveillance-cameras-globally-us-china-amount-citizens

Toomey, Patrick. "The NSA Continues to Violate Americans' Internet Privacy Rights," ACLU, August 22, 2018. https://www.aclu.org/blog/national-security/privacy-and-surveillance/nsa-continues-violate-americans-internet-privacy.

Toor, Amar. "New Database Aims to Track the Global Surveillance Industry," The Verge, August 1, 2016. https://www.theverge.com/2016/8/1/12340348/surveillance-industry-index-database-privacy-international.

Yan, Zhang. "Facial Recognition Used to Track Down Abducted Children," *China Daily*, August 30, 2019. https://www.chinadaily.com.cn/a/201908/30/WS5d6891c9a310cf3e35568c8e.html.

## Websites

**LiveScience** (www.livescience.com/technology) Explore this website's technology section. It contains lots of different articles and activities centered around technology of all kinds.

**National Constitution Center** (constitutioncenter.org/interactive-constitution) Learn about the US Constitution and its amendments that play a role in protecting citizens from unlawful surveillance.

**Stopbullying.gov** (www.stopbullying.gov/resources/kids) Kids are heavily invested in online information and data. This website shows how to keep yourself and others safe from cyberbullying.

**TeensHealth** (kidshealth.org/en/teens/internet-safety.html?ref=search) This website explains how teens can be safe and secure while being online. Learn how to keep private information private, and how to protect again cyberbullying.

# Index

## A

American Civil Liberties Union (ACLU), 8, 22, 26, 82, 85, 102
Amnesty International, 23–27

## B

*Bartnicki v. Vopper*, 95
Bhandari, Vrinda, 61–65
Brandeis, Louis D., 92, 94
Bush, George W., 8

## C

Claridge, Lucy, 24–25
closed circuit television (CCTV), 18, 19, 20, 21, 22, 44, 53
*Cohen v. California*, 94
Cooley, Thomas, 92
*Cox Broadcasting Corp. v. Cohn*, 95

## D

*De Jonge v. Oregon*, 95
Department of Homeland Security, 12, 41, 58, 67, 69
Douglas, William O., 92
Doyle, Aaron, 44
Duggan, Maeve, 28–34

## E

Electronic Frontier Foundation, 79–83

## F

facial recognition technology, 9, 101–104, 105–109
Federal Bureau of Investigation (FBI), 14, 48, 67, 69, 108–109
*Federal Communications Commission v. Pacifica Foundation*, 94
Fifth Amendment, 92
First Amendment, 82, 91–96
*First Unitarian v. NSA*, 82
Fourth Amendment, 8, 15, 82, 83, 92
Future Learn, 52–56

## G

Gans, Joshua, 72–77
*Gilbert v. Minnesota*, 92
*Griswold v. Connecticut*, 92

## H

Haydel, Judith, 91–96
*Hepting v. AT&T*, 82

## I

IP cameras/technology, 19–22

## J

*Jewel v. NSA*, 81–82
Jordan, Jim, 108

**K**

Kasper, Jody, 67, 70–71
Klein, Mark, 80, 81

**L**

Lepeska, David, 40–45
Lepore, Jill, 62
Lowery, Robert, 104
Lynch, Jen, 108

**M**

Maass, Dave, 97–100
Maniam, Shiva, 47–51
Mann, Steve, 72–77
Marshall, Thurgood, 94
McCaney, Kevin, 57–60
Mesnik, Bob, 17–22

**N**

*NAACP v. Alabama*, 95
National Security Agency
   (NSA), 8, 12, 14, 15, 24,
   26, 48, 49, 50, 51, 79–83,
   85, 87, 96
Newman, Bill, 66–71
Ninth Amendment, 92

**O**

Ocasio-Cortez, Alexandria, 108

**P**

*Packer Corporation v. Utah*, 94
Pew Research Center, 7, 14, 15,
   29, 33, 48, 49, 50, 51, 64,
   75, 84–90
Posner, Richard, 12–13

privacy, right to
   found in common law, 92
   found in the US Constitution,
      8, 68, 92
privacy claims, types of, 93
Privacy International, 24,
   26, 35–39
Prosser, Dean William, 93

**R**

Rainie, Lee, 28–34

**S**

Sane, Renuka, 61–65
September 11, 2001, terrorist attacks, 7, 8, 11, 12, 15,
   16, 49, 96
Shaw, C. Mitchell, 11–16
Sheard, Nathan, 105–109
*Shubert v. Obama*, 82
*Smith v. Obama*, 83
Snowden, Edward, 15, 23, 24,
   26, 48, 50, 51, 84, 85, 86, 88
*Stanley v. Georgia*, 94
surveillance
   and fighting crime, 9, 40–44,
      52–56, 57–60
   and fighting terrorism,
      9, 12–16
surveillance industry, 36–39
surveillance technology, history
   and evolution of, 18–20

**T**

Third Amendment, 92

**U**
UK, legal battle over bulk sur-
  veillance practices, 24–27
Urban Institute, 43, 44, 58
USA Patriot Act, 12, 49, 80, 96

**W**
Warren, Samuel D., 92
Wendorf, Marcia, 101–104

# Picture Credits